HOL

EDUCATION

Connecting Head, Heart and Hands

SAMUEL K. BUSULWA

Published by Samuel K. Busulwa and Action Wealth Publishing.

Kemp House
152 -160 City Road
London, EC1V 2NX
United Kingdom

ISBN 978-1-7970-8778-8

Printed and bound in the United Kingdom.

This book is dedicated to my late parents and teachers and to all those who are engaged in educating children

CONTENTS

INTRODUCTION

Anyone who has been in education for a long time will tell you that it becomes part of who you are. You may start out with passion for what you do, but, as the years go by and the experiences mount, the students and the educators become a part of who you are.

A true educator lives the life of education. It is not something they do for a career; it is, rather, something they do as a calling.

I have had many roles in various education streams and through the years, have learned the things that work and those that don't. This is true while dealing with education and in working with people.

I was motivated to write this book in order to share my insights, experiences, and thoughts with others, with the hope that it inspires young educators and motivates students to become teachers.

Without education, a country cannot grow because it is the foundation upon which we build our future. I am honoured to have been a part of cementing foundations for many students and having an influence in their lives. The truth of it is, although I may have had an influence in their lives and for the good, I trust, they have had a marked influence on mine, too.

What follows is the story of a young man who started out believing that he could make a difference, and it tells how he followed his heart, used his head, and put his hands to good use in making his dream of holistic education a reality.

CHAPTER 1

The Young Life of an Educator

My Childhood and Education

All good stories start with the following, and far be it from me to break tradition. I was born on a bright day in September, at Jungo Maternity Centre. I am the ninth child born into a family of twelve children. My parents believed in the importance of education. No wonder I went through my school years at some very good schools: Jungo Primary School, Mengo Junior School, and Bishop Senior Secondary School; that meant my marks were good enough to get me into Old Kampala Senior School, where I did my A' levels.

I've always been aware of the impact my teachers had on my life and studies, and perhaps this input motivated me to become an educator.

My wife, Joyce, was the daughter of my algebra teacher. Going back further than that, my father taught my father-in-law—so academia infiltrated my life on every level.

Every person you speak to will tell you of a teacher who influenced their lives. For me, it was my teacher and headmaster, Thomas Makumbi. One of the things he said to us that has always stuck with me is this: He wouldn't mind if we failed so long as we could think for ourselves.

Allowing learners to have free thought is something I have encouraged in every academic institution I have worked in, and I accredit him with instilling this philosophy in me.

If a student was taken to him for committing an offense, he would expect the student to be honest and able to defend his/her responses. He treated us as individual free thinkers and encouraged us to verbalise our thoughts as well as defend them.

What also impressed me about him was, if we were tasked with manual labour, he would come to school dressed in clothes that allowed him to work alongside us. If we were clearing the bush, he would get a slasher and begin to slash alongside us. His exemplary leadership skills really impressed me, and I have tried to emulate this wherever I have been involved with students.

My junior school headmaster also made an impression on my early years at school. He was also a stickler for time management. He believed that if you couldn't manage your time, you would not be able to manage your life.

He also believed you would not amount to much if you could not do mathematics, however, he also had a lighter side—he would play the organ during morning assembly and tried to teach us how to sing loudly. It was good fun. In that way, he showed me you can be serious and playful while still teaching children.

However, the one thing he never tolerated was tardiness. If you showed up late to school, he'd tell you "don't bother coming in." So, you would be sent home with instructions to come back in the afternoon, where you would be able to make it on time. As an adult, I realised the value of this fixation with time.

As with all children, my parents played a large role in shaping who I became. I have always admired my father and often think about what a good record-keeper he was.

He wrote in his diary every single day, up to the day before he passed away. He made history interesting and was very knowledgeable about what had happened in the past. In this, he taught me that we are all connected and our past influences our present and our future. He was another person who instilled the importance of time management into my life.

If he was to go to Kampala, he would say, "I don't own a car, and the bus does not wait for me, I wait for it." So, he would go to the bus stop before the bus was due and wait, to ensure he did not miss the bus he needed to be on. Something I remember him saying is, "Time does not wait for you. It goes, and you also go, so you can keep up with time."

My mother's gift was that she was very good at making money. Some people just have a knack with it, and she was one of those people.

I remember her making pancakes and things to sell. She would take time to teach me how to make things to sell. She taught me that there is always a way to make money if you need it, as long as you are willing to put in the work. The most important thing she taught me in that area was not only how to make money, but how to make money make money for you.

Having a large family meant I had many brothers and sisters who had an impact on my life as well; I will discuss them slightly later in the book. All in all, I had a good childhood, worked hard, and used my education to start the process of creating a future for myself that would be rewarding.

My Teaching Years

After completing my A levels at Old Kampala School, I joined University of East Africa, Makerere. This was in 1965. Where I completed my first degree, which was a BA Honours. After that, I pursued a Postgraduate Diploma in Education for one year at the same university. When I graduated, I was posted to Bishop's

Senior School, Mukono, where I worked from 1968-1970. In 1971, I was given a scholarship through the Church of Uganda to go to Alexandria, Virginia in the United States to do my master's degree in theology. I was sponsored by Virginia to attend the Teacher's College of Columbia University in New York, where I did a course in Curriculum Design, Development, and Implementation.

When I returned, I was posted to Masaka SS and, in that year 1973, I got married to my late wife, Joyce, who had been at Makerere during the same time. After Makerere, Joyce worked in the Ministry of Finance. She was the first lady to be Deputy Commissioner of the Treasury in Uganda. Later on, she became the Commissioner of the Uganda Treasury and dealt with the budgets. Unfortunately, she passed away, but that was many years later. I fondly remember the good times we had together. Joyce and I had five children, one of whom passed away when he was at University.

Education is important in our family, and we have imparted the love of it to our children. Our first daughter Rachel has a master's degree in Business Administration and has worked in America and Philippines. Christine, our second daughter, studied electrical engineering and is a manager in the Communication Commission. My son Tom is a lawyer based in Kampala, and my youngest daughter, Eva, is also a lawyer and is working with the former Deputy Secretary General in a law firm in Kampala.

I also have young grandchildren who are still in school. I hope their parents' love for education and learning filters down to them. Now, to get back to my teaching years:

From Mukono, I was transferred to Kitante Hill School, where I was appointed Examination Master and then I was posted to Aggrey Memorial

School in 1976 as a headmaster. I think I did a good job there. Aggrey Memorial School became an A-Level school during my time there, and I believe our hard work as staff brought about the desired results in our students.

While there, I oversaw quite a number of developments. There were no staff houses. I built three or four semi-detached houses for the staff. We constructed a playground at the school, and we built two new laboratories in order to have separate labs for physics, chemistry, and biology.

I was then transferred to Mengo Senior School, where I was the headmaster from 1985 to 1988. One outstanding achievement was that I abolished the double-session system.

At the time, Senior 1 and 2 students would attend school in the afternoon, yet another session was held in the morning of the same day. I found this very troublesome and the results were not good either, so there was no reason for advocating to keep a system in place that was clearly not working.

The way the double-session system worked made discipline very difficult to enforce, as well. Teachers were teaching in different schools on the same day, so they would go teach at one school in the morning and appear at another school in the afternoon. Some of them were teaching in three different schools during the course of one day. This did not make sense to me. There was no cohesiveness, and it caused a lot of disruption for the teachers. I set out to find a solution.

My findings were that the school had many workshops and classrooms that were only being used sporadically, and by utilising these rooms properly, we could house the entire student body on one campus without the need to build new classrooms. I'm glad that, later on, even the government adopted the one-campus system and abolished double sessions.

While I was still headmaster at Mengo Senior School, an unexpected turn of events made me a headmaster for King's College Budo. I did not expect it, I was very happy and comfortable at Mengo. I was living in Kololo, which was not far away. This meant I could leave home at a decent time, drive to school in the morning, and go home in the evening. There was no work on the weekends, which meant I had more time with my family.

King's College Budo, on the other hand, was a boarding school, which is twenty-four hours a day, seven days a week of work. It meant I had very little down time. However, as it is my nature, I decided to give my best in my new position.

I was headmaster at Kings College Budo from 1989-2000. While there, we improved the quality of education given at the school. We introduced practical subjects such as electrics and electronics, woodwork, technical drawing, and others. We also rehabilitated the swimming pool. These changes meant we regained the past glory.

We also constructed new structures as well as rehabilitated the existing ones. We bought a new bus and a new pick-up truck for use at the school. Students started playing cricket again, and they were doing very well. Our athletics programme also flourished. Over all, the school rose to the good position that it deserved.

When I was appointed headmaster of King's College Budo, first of all, my predecessor didn't want to leave, he however was sick, and that is why he was recalled to the Ministry headquarters to his substantive post of Assistant Chief Inspector of schools. He was invited by the Minister of Education, together with the Board of Governors, for a meeting. And it was resolved that he had to move to the Ministry headquarters, I was later also invited. One of the interesting questions was, "How are you going to manage Budo? You, who has never studied or worked at Budo?"

I replied, "If Europeans came to Uganda to run Budo, I don't see why a Ugandan who is in Uganda can fail to run Budo. I may not have gone to Budo, but I have a Cambridge Certificate (fortunately, I got a first grade), an Advanced certificate, a BA Honours, and, incidentally, I also have a Master's Degree. If I don't know what academia is, I don't know who does!"

They told me, "Stop there, sir. Don't go any further." Then they asked me another question. "How are you going to handle these students?"

I replied, "I'm not going there to be sectarian. I am going there to run a school. So, my interest is, do they perform well? My friend will be the one who performs well and the one who is there to do the job he's employed to do. It's not he who professes to be born again that should be trusted to do the right thing. I will be interested in seeing their results, regardless of their religious beliefs.

One of the things I did not encourage was for people to come talk to me about others. If they did that, I would say, "Okay, let me invite the person you are speaking about."

I would invite that person to join us and say to them, "Right. Now please repeat what you have to say. If you are not ready to repeat what you told me, then don't tell it to me."

I wanted people to be open and walk in the light, not talking behind the backs of others. I never tolerated backbiting.

Secondly, I insisted on discipline. Before I joined Budo, the levels of discipline had declined. I told them that I would exercise justice but with a firm hand. As I caned the student, I would say, "I am caning you because of this or that."

I may sound harsh, please note, I was strict but fair. That notwithstanding, I became friends with my students. I learned their names and was able to discuss pertinent things with them. I always told my students that we were raising the bar. I would ask them whether they knew how to do a high jump. When they affirmed that they did, I would say that is what we are doing in Budo. Every time I achieved something, we would raise the bar higher and higher to keep bettering ourselves.

Owing to the fact that I interacted a lot with the students, they would come to my house and tell me their problems. I stopped discounting students as difficult or troublesome. Often, a student seen or labelled as difficult has a reason for being out of sorts. Perhaps, he has home life problems or personal problems. So, instead of writing them off as rebellious or difficult, I would say to them, "If you need special attention, we will give you special attention." In addition to giving the students plenty of activities, I permitted them to approach me any time they wanted to do so.

I won the hearts of the students, and the teachers began to understand who I was and how I was working. I wasn't only head of the teachers; I was the leader of the entire school. We worked hard to create a bond that was not only between the students themselves, but between the students and the faculty. Unity is strength, and everyone is important. Those are two important things to remember when working with people, no matter their age.

Learning to differentiate between the categories of students means connecting with the students on different levels. In the same way, a child who goes to school to please his or her parents finds comfort in engaging in examination malpractice at all levels, and then corruption, once they get a job. By understanding why people are at school and university, you will be able to find the point from which to work with them. I found that by keeping my standards high, my expectations constant, and my integrity and honesty at a premium, the students and people I interacted with knew where they stood with me.

This has also been true in my dealings with the Church. I have also been involved in the Church for many years, and I know this has helped me greatly in my work, and my work has helped me greatly with the Church.

I am a Church Warden, in the capacity as a member of the diocese synod and also in the capacity on the council, as a delegate to the provincial assembly for the Church of Uganda. I am also a member of the consortium court.

Through this, I learned to keep the secrets of the Church concerning all confidential matters. This has improved my confidentiality, even in other aspects of life. This also helped me as a Chief Examiner, as you are not allowed or expected to share results when they are not yet officially released, even if the results are those of your own children. This taught me to be a man of integrity.

Integrity got me chosen as the chairperson of the worship committee that was responsible for the coronation of the current King of Buganda, Kabaka Ronald Muwenda Mutebi. I am proud of being the Chairman of the Cardinals, Bishops, and Archbishops, who also sat on that committee.

Being a treasurer in the Church meant that the Church entrusted me with their finances. This helped me to withstand all the problems that confront a treasurer and also to withstand the religious leaders, as you stick to the truth on how church money is meant to be spent. Being able to stand your ground is very important in all walks of life, no matter what area of work you find yourself in.

My contribution to the Church is honesty. Honesty to myself and to my religious leaders. Not to hide the truth from them, especially during decision making. You are there to listen and to maintain your impartiality. You must listen to both sides before passing judgment; this was also my practice with school discipline, where I would listen to the student and the teacher rather than the teacher alone. I think the students appreciated my giving them a fair hearing, and it often gave the teacher a greater insight into the student's motives.

I stayed at Budo until I retired. I still have many students from King's College who get in touch with me and fondly remember their time there. For me, that is always a good indication that we, as the staff and teachers, did our job well.

No sooner had I retired from Budo than I was invited by the late Professor William Senteza Kajubi, who was Vice Chancellor of Nkumba

University, to become the University's first full-time Academic Registrar. I worked in Nkumba for nine years.

When I retired from Nkumba, the Vice Chancellor of Ndejje University invited me to Ndejje to start new courses at Ndejje University, especially at the Kampala campus. The courses I started were in computer science with education and early childhood education. These courses led to an increase in the intake at the University, I am pleased to say.

I was there until 2014, when I felt my work had been done and I could leave it in the capable hands of the staff and lecturers.

I have a smile on my face when I think back on all those years; teaching and leading educational professionals. I would like to think I have had a significant impact on student's lives and hope they have gone on from strength to strength.

***

Coming from a big family and having older brothers and sisters was very enjoyable. My older siblings always came back from school during holidays and told us stories about boarding school life, how it was a lot of fun, and its academic demands. This inspired me to work hard in order to go to a boarding school some day and be like them, so I could tell the same stories to others. The people one grows up around—not only your family, but also neighbours, teachers, and friends—can be very influential in one's life. I am very grateful for the people in mine who left such a warm, indelible mark on my childhood.

Looking Ahead

Today, I may have left the education system, but it is in my blood and is my passion. With that in mind, I started a consultancy that deals with the training of teachers for schools, and providing workshops to teachers on management and designing of school curriculum. My interest in this came while I was still a headmaster. At that time, I was also a member of the National Curriculum Development Centre.

During that time, I was sponsored to attend a course at the University of Mauritius dealing with Curriculum Design, Development, and its Implementation. I learned a lot, as it was a very elaborate and informative course. When I came back, starting as far back as when I was headmaster at Budo, we wrote and designed our own school curriculum. In doing so, we could tailor-make the curriculum to suit the students and teachers' strengths. Different groups of children, studying in schools in different areas, need different education. We also found, by writing our own curriculum, we could enhance the way it was taught and learned.

That is what I do now through the consultancy. What we aim to achieve is what a school curriculum is, in its basic form. This means looking at what you are trying to teach the students and how it should be done. We look at how to design teaching materials that will effectively engage the students and motivate the teachers. We do this by making sound lesson plans and marking schemes that the teachers can use.

What we found was, in the past, many teachers just used previous exam papers, duplicated questions from them, and gave those questions to students. Also, students would be reviewing and trying to look at past questions and then memorising the questions and their answers. This created a situation where the students were just memorising what they needed to, in order to pass the exams, and not actually understanding the content of the work.

What was happening was, if students were asked slightly different questions from a previous year, they wrote down everything they remembered about the subject. This then led to the examiner circling their work and commenting that what they had answered was irrelevant. Not wrong, but irrelevant as pertaining to the question asked on the test. This caused the students to get lower marks.

We found that we needed to create a platform that allowed the students to understand the work, be able to read and answer what was being asked; instead of listing every tree in the forest, they could answer with what trees are at the perimeter of the forest, for example. You see, many teachers try to train students to write model answers based on previous questions. There is no such thing as a model answer. It will not get you good marks. It will make you a critical thinker.

That is my emphasis and where my passion lies in training teachers to create students who understand their work, think about the questions asked, and write an appropriate answer.

To have enough understanding to be able to differentiate between a question asking you to list the trees in the forest and one that asks for a list of trees around the perimeter of the forest. This is a hyperbolic example, but it does get the point across.

I am also keen on a concept known as Teaching Moments. This is where the teacher sees the opportunity to use what is around him or her to teach what needs to be taught. Also, for teachers to not tell stories that may divert students' attention. The students remember the story but not the content.

Those are things we are dealing with these days. Things like teamwork in a school. How can you have an entire school moving in the same direction? How do you bring the teachers, students, and faculty in the direction you want the school to move in? How do you keep a healthy level of respect between the students and teachers, yet create a cohesive school body?

How can the school interpret the school motto in teaching? If Mengo says, *"Akwana Akira Ayomba,"* (make friends and not foes) how is it relevant to the education you are getting? Or if Gayaza says, "Never Give Up," how do you rate it to your daily work?

Or when Budo says, *"Gakyali Mabaga"*? (so much to do, so little done) That is very interesting, because it's telling you that you have not reached your destination. Whatever you have achieved—*Gakyali Mabaga* (so much to do, so little done). And the students realised, when you score 100%, it is still Gakyali Mabaga. It is not the be-all and end-all. There is more to do, more to learn, more to achieve.

Nabbingo says, "Be True." What does it mean to the daily work of the students and even the teachers?

Many schools have mottos but they have not internalised what the founders meant by the mottos. Ideally, mottos give students the philosophy of the school and something to strive towards. We all need goals set for us so we may collectively strive to achieve them.

My focus now is to achieve these things and much more. Education is the foundation for adulthood. Therefore, educators have a pivotal role in not only teaching children the curriculum, but teaching them and guiding them on how to be good, hard-working, functional, and successful adults.

I can't think of a worthier career to have chosen, and I am blessed to still be able to have an input into teachers' and students' lives.

CHAPTER 2

Teaching

The Old Ways

Many people think, and it is often more prevalent in youth, that the "old ways" should be discarded and have no value in modern times. I disagree with this thinking. Yes, there are some aspects that need to be disregarded, I do agree. One of these is the mindset about girls' and women's education. However, there were many merits in the old teaching ways that have been lost in today's education system, and we are poorer for it.

The teaching methods of Africa were based on demonstration and learning by doing. A new concept was first demonstrated then taught, and finally it was practiced by the student until perfection was achieved.

The education in the past was aimed at creating skill sets, therefore emphasis was on skills like clothes making, blacksmithing, hunting, construction, and learning about trading. Some of the Ugandan education systems allowed children to be sent to the King's Court. This was done in order for them to learn how to debate, dispense justice, hear, listen, and understand what they were hearing, as well as learn how to deliver a message clearly and succinctly. Children were taught about obedience and were trained in what was necessary and expected of them in order to serve the royal elders.

They were also trained to be security conscious about what dangers may present themselves and how to deal with them. It was a cultural- and practical-based education system.

They did not only teach skills but also values and social etiquette. For example, some of the areas that were taught were humility, patience, manners, apologizing, greeting, silence while eating, deportment, respect for elders, social etiquette, critical thinking, and the weighing of what to say and when to say it.

Students were taught to be productive, not to be idle, as an idle mind is the workshop of the devil. Taboos were not superstitions back then; more, they were the things we were not supposed to do, based on safety and security.

Examples of these were:

> Do not sweep at night—this was not because some evil spirit would come and take you away; it was because it

was not safe to be outside alone at night.

➢ Do not go to the well at noonday. This may seem odd, but it was a practical suggestion to avoid succumbing to the heat of the day, due to the hard labour of carrying water when the sun is at its hottest.

➢ Don't walk around alone at night—this one was especially taught to the young girls.

➢ A father-in-law should not shake hands with his daughter-in-law and vice versa.

➢ Do not give birth out of wedlock.

➢ Be productive in your community.

➢ Work hard and be grateful for the work you have.

➢ Show your elders respect and they will respect you back.

These are just a few examples of the social aspect of what was taught.

The Value of the Old Ways

The benefits were that children were taught useful skills as well as moral values. They created a well-rounded student who not only learned skills to enable them to do work that would put food on the table, but also how to interact with respect and decency as adults.

Rules and regulations are not there to restrict all behaviour; only unacceptable or dangerous behaviours. I think today we need a more holistic approach to what we teach our children, in order for them to be able to function better in a complicated and competitive world as adults.

In our education system today, we need to teach our children that these so-called taboos are not evil, but are actually for their own good. I believe, if you tell a student "why" and not just "what," you give them understanding; you don't just expect them to accept what they are being told. If you tell a teenage student, "Don't sweep outside at night," she may dismiss that advice as archaic and ridiculous. However, if you say to her, "Don't sweep at night outside, as this makes you visible and vulnerable to any bad element that may be lurking around," you are giving her the "why", and with that, are giving her an understanding of the reason behind the taboo.

In the same way, if you tell someone, "Don't marry your brother, sister, or first cousin," they may think you are being old fashioned and trying to destroy their happiness. However, if you say to them, they shouldn't marry their brother, sister, or cousin as the similarity in their DNA, their genetic makeup, can cause serious birth defects and possible mental retardation in the children they may have, you have given them sound scientific grounding for the taboo, which makes it much easier to understand.

A lot of the old values were about respect, honesty, morals, and integrity. These have, in a lot of ways, lost their place in today's education system and have been replaced by more modern trends. By losing these values, we are only educating our children in part, as we are not giving them a balanced and well-rounded education that will allow them to thrive in the adult world.

That is why we now need to have a senior woman teacher for the girls and a senior man teacher for the boys in every school, to teach this social education. We cannot just expect it to be taught at home. There are many children who live with other family members or have a parent who works far away, and, due to that, they miss out on this aspect of education. It then becomes the school's place to give it to them.

A New Approach

It is with this thinking that a new approach needs to be adopted. We need to look at education holistically, encompassing the head, heart, and hands. In this way, we will create balanced, well-rounded students who are well equipped, educationally and emotionally, to step confidently into the adult and business world, post schooling.

In Budo, we came up with a program called Child to Child Education. This was where senior students would go and speak to the junior students regarding social issues such as sex education.

As this was not done elsewhere that we were aware of, we came up with our own syllabus, inviting different specialists in different social areas to speak to the students. We had counsellors, medical doctors, and health care professionals. We also encouraged an open Q&A,

in order for the children to get answers to questions they couldn't ask their parents, and also in order for them to get factual answers.

By doing this, we believed we created honesty between us and the children. It gave us a platform to interact with them on a more social and personal level. They understood we cared not just for their educational well-being, but also for their emotional and health well-being.

One of the most important things children must know is that they are created equal, even though they are different. It is important for them to know they all have different gifts and they all have talents. We encouraged teachers to seek out the individual talents and gifts in each child and help them improve on them. This gave, and gives, the child a sense of self-worth that they can be proud of.

Teachers need to improvise visual aid teaching materials, since the method of teaching today is mostly classroom-based. We have found that students connect better when they can read and see something, rather than just try to imagine it in their heads. This creates a better recall of the subject matter when needed.

Record-keeping is also a very key element in teaching children. Children live in the present, but we, as adults, have a deeper understanding about how the past is connected to the present. By teaching children, the value of the past, and not just with regards to social history but with regards to their own lives, we teach them that things of value need to be looked after. They may not be here forever. This pertains to people as much as to material things and moments.

Today's way is to use and throw away, so we need to know that keeping things is the source of wealth. We need to teach children that maintenance is far better than making new things all the time. It is far cheaper to repair than to replace. There are some things you can't replace, such as relationships.

Teaching children to keep records about their lives will allow them to look back and see how far they have come and how much they have grown. Another benefit is that writing what they are feeling at the time means they will put themselves into a different headspace. This often allows a better understanding of a problem and perhaps can encourage them to seek help, if they need it.

My Open-Door Policy

With what we have discussed in the previous section, you will understand why I initiated my Open-Door Policy. This was where the students and teaching staff could, at any time, come to talk to me about anything that was worrying them or even just about something they wanted to discuss.

To understand people, you have to speak to them and engage them. It does not work for a school principal to be aloof, as he will never understand his students. As I previously said, being able to connect with students gives you an understanding of the motives for their actions. Too often, I have seen children ostracized for bad behaviour without the cause or the influence being investigated.

Perhaps a student is constantly late for school, so the teacher does not allow him in class. What this achieves would be to teach a child who is lazy and won't get out of bed in the morning a lesson on the importance of time management. However, it won't help the child who is constantly late because she has to get her four younger siblings up, fed, dressed, and to their schools before she can come to school herself.

Do you see the difference understanding a situation holistically makes? What an Open-Door

Policy does is allow the child who battles to get out of bed in the morning to come to you and tell you he feels so tired in the mornings that, although he tries to get up on time, he simply can't. That gives you the opportunity to try and help him. Perhaps he is not going to bed early enough; perhaps he is going to bed hungry and sleeping badly, as his stomach is not full. Perhaps his parents fight all night, and he cannot get enough rest. Never think unilaterally when dealing with people, especially children. Their lives are not always as easy as we perceive them to be.

Creating an Open-Door Policy works both ways. The child learns to respect the teacher, because he realises that the concern is care, and he is not simply going to be in trouble again. It creates understanding and a wider scope of opportunity for help and education for the teacher.

The benefits of this type of human-to-human interaction as opposed to "teacher on a platform and child on the ground" thinking creates a connection between teachers and students. The result is that the student feels important and heard. This will bring about marked changes in their attitude toward work. In the same way an employee who feels valued will give his best, a student who feels heard and understood will give their best. This is because they know, if something goes wrong, they are not going to get into trouble, but can instead reach out and get help.

Feeling alone is a terrible emotion to carry around. I tried to ensure that everyone I worked with knew that if I was there, they were never alone. There was always someone to listen to them who would genuinely try to help them in whatever way I could.

However, when they did wrong or harmed another person, if they were unethical or immoral, my punishment was meted out after I explained to them why it was being done and how their behaviour could not be condoned. I always wanted to be seen as fair but just. Students did not get away with bad behaviour, but they always had the opportunity to explain why it occurred.

The students we have in our care are the leaders, doctors, lawyers, parents, and teachers of tomorrow. Teaching them to be fair but just and to talk about things means that they, in turn, will be fair and just to their patients, clients, children, and students down the line.

Teaching Begins at Home

This section is twofold. First, what happens at home is brought to the classroom, so educators need to take that into account when working through problems with learners, realizing a situation may have longer reaching causes than meet the eye.

As with the example I used about the student who was consistently late due to having to get her siblings up and ready, when you take the time to find out the why, not just the what, you will more likely come across a reason, not an excuse.

Home life cannot be left at home. Children do not have the shut-off valve that adults do. What happens at home is carried on their shoulders and will always have an effect in the classroom. If the students feel they can speak to you about it, it gives you the opportunity to initiate a change that may change the student's life. If you know that getting four siblings up and ready is damaging the student's education, you can speak to the student about perhaps having a meeting with their parents, to try and eliminate the cause. Sometimes it is as easy as that—the parents don't realise the effect it is having on the child, and, once they do, a solution is found that eliminates the problem.

Sometimes it is not so easy, and social services or family members may be necessary to help the child. Children are vulnerable, even the older ones. They need our experience, help, and guidance to create strong children who grow into strong adults. Educators are often that bridge. By seeing a child's heart, you can then educate their minds and guide their hands.

Secondly, what happens in the classroom needs to be translated back to the home. This means that learning must start at the level of understanding for the learner where they are, and from there you can grow their knowledge. Each child is different and needs to be treated as such.

Let me use an example. I may like jam sandwiches for my lunch. My staff would be very unhappy if everyone had to have jam sandwiches because I do. Perhaps some like ham sandwiches or cheese, or perhaps some don't even like sandwiches. In the same way, you can't lump children together.

Each child comes from a different background, has been raised in a different way, and is a different person. By allowing them their individualism, you give them a sense of self that fosters a pride in who they are and what they are good at.

Educators have an important role, not just in imparting knowledge, but in leading by example. This means they have to be kind, firm, understanding, and still balanced enough to create order and discipline in the classroom. This shows the student how a balanced and good society works, and they will be able to take that home with them.

We have to teach children to respect themselves, their fellow students, and the teaching staff. Then, they will go home and respect their parents, friends, and siblings.

Discipline has to be constant, though, because when something is wrong, it is wrong. Children, whether at home or at school, must know there are lines they cannot cross. Stealing, cheating, fighting, and lying are the four that spring to mind.

An Open Door does not mean a soft touch. My students knew that about me. They could speak to me about anything, but it didn't always mean they would not get in trouble for it.

Sometimes the only boundaries and social education a child gets are from their schoolmates and their teachers. It is a great responsibility to be a teacher, as you have to be a parent, educator, and disciplinarian all rolled into one.

Always remember: you cannot educate a mind if the heart and hands have not been engaged. A three-legged pot cannot stand on one leg.

Be wise in your dealings with your students, and when in doubt, speak to other professionals, as often two minds are better than one. Another educator may give you a different perspective that will help you find a solution.

Create a classroom that makes the student want to come to school. Make it a place where they can learn, discuss, and be heard. This will translate back into their home lives and will give them a foundation that will change their lives forever.

Teach at the Correct Level of the Child

We don't teach algebra to a six-year-old, and we don't teach reading to a Year 6 student. In the same way the curriculum is based on where the student is academically, you need to interact and create understanding in education that is pegged at a student's level.

Each child is different, and you may need to adapt your work accordingly. It is no good having lengthy discussions about online market trading to children who come from a community that farms. By putting the fiscal example into terms they understand, such as cattle, farming, and produce, you bring it to a level that makes sense to them.

Having said that, you may have one child or a group of them who do understand international financial markets. This goes back to what I said about getting in additional outside people to reach children where they are or asking a teacher who is well-versed in this area to spend time with these students. It will have a great impact on them if this is not your field.

Using examples that students can relate to, whatever they may be, brings education into life. It links the two, and once you have connected the outside world with your classroom, your children will be able to take your classroom into the outside world.

CHAPTER 3

Collectivism Versus Individualism

Working Towards Your Place in the Sun

Everybody has to, essentially, make it in the world alone. You may have support, but in the end, it is up to you to make something of yourself. This is something that needs to be taught to students. Their future is in their hands. It is not going to be handed to them by someone else. It is up to them to study hard to create a life and a living for themselves. As the saying goes, *Hard work never broke any bones.*

I have added this chapter into this part of the book because teaching the difference between the two is integral to the core of educating children.

We need to teach students that they have to work for what they want. There is no fairy godmother who is going to wave a wand and give it to them. If you look at everyone who has achieved something great, you will see a history of hard work, time spent, and failures. The reason they succeeded is that they never gave up and they continued to work towards their goals, by themselves and for themselves.

This is how you achieve your place in the sun.

That sounds like individualism, but it is not the only way to achieve goals. There are two schools of thought about how to achieve goals: Individualism and Collectivism. Let's take a moment to look at the differences between the two.

Individualism

The premise of individualism is that your goals supersede those of the people around you. You focus on *your* needs and what *you* want to achieve more than what is good for the group.

This has pros and cons. The pros being that you are self-sufficient, self-motivated, and self-reliant. There is no one else to blame when things go wrong; individualism teaches you self-responsibility. The cons are it is tough to do it all alone. It is hard to always be the one who has to do anything that has to be done or that you want to achieve. There is no buddy system to relieve you and motivate you. It can cause arrogance against people who are collectivists.

Collectivism

The premise for collectivism is that the goals of the *group* are more important than your own individual goals. You work as part of a whole to achieve a goal together.

The pros are that you have support and can rely on others' experience in an area to help move the group closer to the goal. It means you have people to rely on, lean on, bounce ideas off, and get help from. It can propel you forward faster, as there are many people who are working together to get things done.

The cons are that you lose your individuality and have to put your goals aside or bring them in line with the group's. It is also sometimes used as a way of not taking responsibility when things go wrong, as there are others on whom you can lay the blame. It can also mean that people are less motivated and feel less proud of what the group has achieved.

So, which is the right one: individualism or collectivism? The answer is *both*. You achieve balance by learning to work as an individual in a collective group. This is why it is imperative for educators to teach their students the benefit of both collectivism and individualism, as well as how to identify when one is needed over the other.

Teaching students that they need to conform to collectivism whilst still maintaining their individualism seems like an idea at odds with itself. How can you teach a student to be self-reliant while teaching them to lean on their fellow students? The answer is simple. Teach the student they are important as an individual, that their problems, ideas, and goals for themselves are what they need to focus on; however, they need to work within a group for the greater good. You can keep your own goals at the fore, but in school and in life, you will always have to work with people.

By using individualism within a collective workspace, you can still keep your own goals and be your own person. If you are tasked with a job within the group and you have a strong time management ethic, you can keep your individual personal ethic and do your part in the time span allotted. The same can be said for quality, as often one student does more in a group than another. Individualism allows you to do your best, regardless of what another person does, because it is about you and your effort and your goals.

Keeping your individuality within a collective group is about sticking to who you are—not just your goals, but your personal ethics, morals, and motivation.

Together We Are Stronger

Teach students that, whilst they have to work for their place in the sun, they have to balance that with knowing no man is an island. We may have to put in the work ourselves, but we don't have to do it alone. Teaching students about the strength in teamwork and unity creates bonds and allows the students to grow stronger together. You have to make it on your own, but not alone.

There is a lot to be said about teamwork. It creates a lively work environment. Team members learn to work with and around others; they learn comradery and how to hone their people skills in order to get the job done and achieve the goal.

There is also the benefit of achieving something with a group that binds them together. Take war veterans, for example. Their collective experiences form a bond between soldiers for life. Why do people have school reunions? People go to school reunions because the bond they shared while at school remains strong.

Collectivism and individualism are not opposite entities. Individualism can slot into collectivism and not be altered. However, for a person who does not have a strong individual core and is only used to working collectively, being thrust into an adult world where individualism is vital can be a make-or-break situation. That is why we need to treat our students as individual people, not just collective students.

We need to let the child contribute to what he or she wants to study. We need to prepare teachers to be more child-centred and not teacher-centred, to help the people they teach to discover themselves.

What is of paramount importance is to allow the educators to teach their students to make a life and to make a living. To make a life is to know who you are individually and also how you fit into being one of many. It is about teaching them what their position and role is on this planet of ours in relation to others. You are not created to live in isolation, but you have to learn to work for your own goals whilst still being part of and working towards the goals of a group.

Do you remember, when we were at school, and it still happens today, we were told to cover our work, so our neighbours didn't copy what we were doing? I feel this is too individualistic and hampers teaching students the benefits of collectivism. We should be concerned more with sharing and teaching the students how two heads are often much better than one.

When students work in groups, I have seen how they spark new ideas and creativeness that may not have happened if the student was working alone. Having people to bounce ideas off often brings about results that could not be foreseen at the start. This happens because, when you brainstorm in a group, other people's perspectives and ideas give you fresh insight into a subject, and that, in turn, allows your brain to go off on new tangents that bring new ideas. Then, those new ideas do the same for someone else. This leads to innovative thinking, problem solving on a different and elevated level, and advanced outcomes.

It is a fine balance between teaching students to remain individuals and having them work in groups. There are often times that educators need to monitor students and adjust the balance between individual work time and group work time, depending on the student's nature.

For students who work best and prefer to work on their own, giving them some projects and work to do in a group will allow them to learn new skills they may not utilise by always working on their own. The converse is true for students who prefer to work in a group—they need to be given work that has to be done individually, as they need to learn to rely on their own intuition and carry the responsibility of the work on their shoulders.

This is part of the premise for holistic education: creating well-rounded students who can excel in both individual and collective environments.

The Educator's Role as a Pivot

The educator plays a key role as a pivot between collectivism and individualism. As an educator, you have to teach your students to balance the desire to succeed as an individual with the prospective growth that comes from working as a team. We will discuss how to grow students who know the time for both.

We, as educators, are here to help students learn to be an individual, but we also must help them to remember they are not walking this journey alone. Hence, the principle of sharing.

Also, in a school system, there is what you call distributed leadership. In a structured school system, you may have monitors in a classroom and prefects who oversee more than one class of students or the entire student body. This distributed leadership system is the English model we are currently using. It also works with the educators and facilitators. You have a class teacher, you have a department, you have a deputy, you have a principal. You have all these levels of responsibility in order to help you collectively achieve what you want to achieve, as a school.

What we need to see is, for example, the specialist in infant education or early childhood education being given room to exercise what he or she knows best. Simply because you are the head of a school does not mean you are a specialist in early childhood education.

Drawing on the strengths of your educators will enhance the collective strength and outcomes of the school as a whole. Allow your staff to do what they are trained to do, in the area in which they are trained to do it.

I also believe in hands-on education. This is a good way to teach both individualism and collectivism. It doesn't make much sense to teach agriculture when you have no farm or garden where the students can grow plants or produce, especially in Africa. That's why schools used to have demonstration farms, plots, or gardens, so their students could get their hands dirty, dig in the ground, and learn about growing produce from seed to harvest.

That means, the design of the institutional environment is also important. How we construct our classrooms, ventilation, chairs—all these things must be taken note of and their value understood.

I once visited a college in Canada. For them, the roof was their practical room. They didn't put up a ceiling when they were constructing the building, as they used the exposed roofing structure to teach their students. They were able to understand what trusses, bearers, battens, roof sheet overlaps, etc. were, because they could see them right above their heads. It made me see the value in using what is around us to aide educating our students. We should not cover up those things that can be used to demonstrate our syllabus.

I believe in exposing children to a variety of experiences, so they may learn through all the experiences. Every experience has something to teach a student. By limiting the experiences, you are limiting their growth.

This is why I am delighted to see that schools are going back to sports days, where the balance of individualism and collectivism is played out so well. A student may run against another student in the sprint race, but he will have to work with that same opponent in the relay race. What a wonderful way to show students that you can be an individual but still work collectively.

I am also happy to see that open days are happening at more schools. These are days where parents may come into the school and are shown around by the teachers or students, who explain what is happening in the children's work, what areas they are studying, and what they have achieved on their own and in their groups.

Some schools have drama and music days. I would like to see more of these happening, as they are very important. Again, the students have the opportunity to showcase their talents and skills to their parents. Some schools have debates and quizzes between classes and between different schools. This will quickly form a collective bond, as the students become protective and proud of their school and want their team to do well.

Competition is a good thing; it allows students to showcase what they have learned. Being proud of what you have achieved is not a bad thing. It is a good thing, and we should encourage it in our students. It will motivate them to push themselves further and onward.

If we put emphasis on these, they will be very useful to the students and educators. The bond between them will be strengthened as they all work towards the same goal.

After all, when students go out into the adult world, they need to communicate what they are doing and what they plan to do. As such, it is important for educators to teach children to express themselves in a variety of ways. If we don't teach a child drama or debate, they will not have the confidence to stand on a stage or a platform and speak to people. These are things we do that are not immediately examinable, but they help you to make it in life. Just because they are not examinable does not mean they are not important.

When you look back at your school life, you may not remember how to find x in an algebraic equation, but perhaps you will remember the football you played or the swimming or the debate, the athletics or scouting. That's where we should put our emphasis, as well.

We have created a system of holistic education that ensures our students are well-rounded when they leave our schools. Giving them the skills to work as individuals as well as in groups. There is so much more than educating simply for an exam result.

We, as educators, need to bring our teaching methods into the modern age. We need to realise that we are not just pumping facts and figures, history and mathematics, science and art into our students. We have the privilege of helping them become well-rounded, not only in academia, but emotionally, mentally, intellectually, and physically. There is no greater gift you can give a child than the best tools to become a well-rounded, capable adult. That is the gift of holistic education.

CHAPTER 4

Educating in a Modern World

A nybody who lives with modern teenagers will notice that they have evolved to have an additional appendage: their mobile phone.

I joke, but the mobile phone has become such a part of the lives of our youth that we cannot and should not write it off as something that should be banned from the classroom. I would rather suggest that use of technology, whether it be mobile phones or the Internet, can create interest in a subject for students and, also, reach them on a level they understand.

Incorporating Technology

We are busy punishing students when they come to school with their mobile phones. This creates a separation and bigger distance between the educator and student. The student thinks the educator is old school, someone who doesn't understand modern technology, and often they are correct.

Instead of demonizing something, bring it into the classroom and using it for educational purposes. By doing so, the educator creates a bridge across the age/technology rift that currently exists.

What we should be looking at virtual learning as the way forward in education. The question is: How do we use mobile phones, tablets, and computers to teach so children will learn at their own pace? By answering these questions, we take that step forward into the space where our youth exist today.

Another benefit is that the teacher can teach the students how to research and find their own answers to questions they have, moving the educator away from being the centre of learning and into becoming the facilitator of self-learning.

Each student in a classroom has an idea, a thought, and an answer. How many students don't participate because they don't want to stand out in the crowd? How do you reach that boy or girl at the back of the classroom?

Let's take history, for example. Imagine you are teaching the history of Uganda and say, "Who can find out, using the Internet, who the first King of Uganda was?"

Suddenly, it is no longer a history lesson, but you have brought finding answers into the modern age. I guarantee you every student will be scouring the Internet to find the answer. You have shifted history from being boring to being super cool. This is a very simple example, but it does show you how easy it is to take something that needs to be learned and make it something the student are excited to answer.

I know you are going to ask me, "Where will you get the money from to have these things in the hands of children?" There are many ways of achieving this. As with anything in life, if you have the will, you will find a way. Our leaders have promised laptops for scholars, which is a big step forward. They are aware that knowledge abounds everywhere, so learners/students can learn at their own pace by finding the answers themselves, instead of being spoon-fed.

The ultimate aim of an educator is to teach your students to think for themselves, to rationalise, and to want to search for answers. What better way to do this than through the utilisation of modern technology? This is taking education into their era and bringing it to life for them.

What it also achieves is to prepare the student for adulthood by giving them the tools and skills to be able to find answers later in life, when there is no educator around to give them the answers.

This is a life skill, and too often in education today these are not addressed as the necessities they are. Using modern technology creates an ability to acquire knowledge, wherever you are and whenever you need it. The world today is run virtually. We send letters that aren't written on paper and are sent via airwaves. We link to people in other countries using the Internet, and we can gain access to any information we need without leaving our chairs. What modern technology does is give you a world of resources at your fingertips. This is a huge bonus for educators, as well as for students.

Having an educator available in order to find help in a difficult area has been eradicated, as the answer can be found by using the Internet and doing the legwork yourself. Technology is actually an enabler rather than the disabler we have deemed it.

It will teach the student not only how to find answers, as I said before, but more than that, it will teach the student to think for themselves, to use critical thinking, and to follow a process until they reach the answers they need.

Students will also learn a lot of other things along the way. As you know, when you search for something on the Internet, you always find interesting facts and bits of knowledge along the way. What this may do for some students is open their eyes to the wonderful knowledge the Internet offers—far above social media and posting selfies.

I have left the most important benefit until last. Modern technology takes the responsibility of learning and shares it with the student. It makes the student a part of the education process, of the acquiring knowledge process, instead of just being the recipient.

Every educator knows how uplifting it is when your students are engaged in the subject you are teaching. Now, we can create waves of enthusiasm in every subject by using the Internet to connect the classroom to the world.

Utilising Technology

Something that is not always realised is, by utilising the available technology, you have access to the greatest minds in the world. Do you want to know what the moon landing was about? Watching the video on YouTube will make it stick in the student's mind much more than reading about it will. Do you want to explain how climate change is affecting the world? Watching Greenpeace videos and reading about the awareness they are trying to achieve and how they are going about it will make it personal.

Ecology, geology, sociology, democracy, sports, healthcare—you name it, there is something on the Internet that will make the subject visual for students. Discussing snow with children who have never seen it and asking them to imagine what it is like to live for four months of the year trapped in your house because you are snowed in is asking a lot. But by showing them video clips of actual people who live like this and showing them photos of what a metre of snow in your garden looks like will make it real.

Watching a real-time newsfeed of a natural disaster, such as Hurricane Edna, creates a greater impact than saying that roofs have been blown off and the sea is crashing over the roads.

Usage of modern technology should be a tool encouraged by teachers. It will broaden both the teacher's capacity to educate as well the students' understanding. It can bring the entire world's body of knowledge to both the educator and student.

Further to this, by utilising the Internet and Skype, one teacher who is proficient in a subject has the ability to reach many students, no matter where they are. Virtual classrooms can be used to educate many children in various places at once.

Now, using the new website engine, you can access the best mathematics teacher wherever he is. And with students in Uganda, maybe scattered in different schools, you can find someone who has mastered that topic and do virtual education. Wouldn't that be great? We should explore and exploit the technology for our benefit, as well as for the students'.

What it will do is allow us to educate children using excellent educators where they may not have access to them under different circumstances.

I don't know about you, but this makes me very excited. We have the opportunity to reach children and link them to fellow students in other parts of the country, much like the old pen-pal letter-writing way we did when we were young.

It also means that one educator can reach and teach many students. We have a shortage of teachers, and this is a relatively simple solution to address that. No longer do you need the children to be *in* the classroom. They can gather in twenty different locations and all be taught by one person. This could revolutionise education in Uganda and, indeed, in every African country.

You could get the greatest teachers in their field from any country to educate children all over Africa. All it needs is planning and motivation. Most educators I know are full of both.

I am by no means saying that technology should replace traditional education. I am advocating it be used as an additional tool to bring education to life and give it a global dimension that is often lacking through words on a page.

For example, using a game to explain basic geometry will make it more appealing and easier to understand than watching a teacher drawing triangle on a blackboard. Finding educational programmes that make the student use their critical and rational thinking processes will help them understand the subject so much more and grow their problem-solving skills as much as they're gaining knowledge.

Imagine being able to take your students on a virtual tour of the observation deck of the Empire State Building or of Mount Everest? I don't know of a person who wouldn't find that engaging.

However, technology can teach more than straight education. It can be used to teach social and life skills.

Another area where it creates a good impact is by teaching children about social responsibility. What does your social media footprint say about you? What are you portraying to the outside world? Is this the type of person you want others to think you are?

I believe, to teach and educate holistically, you have to gain access to students' lives. This is something you cannot force; you have to earn their respect and allow them to open up to you. We are more than educators. Often, we spend more time with students than their parents do, which makes us their emotional, spiritual, and educational guardians for the time they are in our care.

Social responsibility is also important to learn because many prospective employers will look at a potential employee's social media to ascertain what type of person they really are. The candidate may believe it is easy to act responsibly in an interview, but if their Facebook page shows them constantly drunk and getting into fights, or having racial, radical political, or social tenancies, they are not the type of person who is going to become employed.

Using technology such as the Internet opens the door to teaching children what it means to be a functioning and acceptable member of society. Whilst their private life is just that—private—it will have an impact on their work and career life, which is why potential employers use this tool.

Another good use for mobile phones is to create work groups set up in WhatsApp. This links all the relevant students, whether a few or the entire class, and allows them to communicate about a topic, even when they are not together. Often, students live far apart or do not have transportation to get together after school to work on a project. A group such as I've described allows them to work together virtually and share information.

I want to say one thing: if you wait for this big animal called government, it will take you ages to change. Each school, I believe, with an enlightened administration, can bring these changes to their classrooms. Some schools already have virtual classrooms. Governments should visit those schools to learn a lesson or two.

So, let schools collaborate more, if they want change, rather than wait for change to come from above. Reforms initiated from above do not normally take effect unless and until the teachers are on board.

So, from the bottom to the top. It is about being the change and creating the change you want to see.

These are but a few of the thousands of ideas available to the educator who is willing to do some research and incorporate technology into the classroom.

Think Globally, Act Locally

This is a well-known adage, but what it means to me is twofold.

Firstly, it means, especially we Africans in our African countries on our African continent, we tend to live and think locally. We have been let down in the past, perhaps, or are lacking in confidence to believe we have what it takes to be global players.

Africa is at the point of change, and it is the continent the rest of the world is watching. What better way to showcase our growth than in the education of our youth? These are the leaders of tomorrow, and we have the opportunity to shape them now.

Thinking globally means we must be aware of what is happening around the world, if we want to have an impact on it. The mindset that we can't have an impact on it is changing, and so it should. We have great minds, strong leaders, innovation, and incredibly clever academics and entrepreneurs. We have the potential to be a big player globally, and it all starts locally.

To create a world player, he needs to grow strong locally first. We educators, alongside parents, have the greatest influence on the people who are going to be our leaders, doctors, professors, CEOs, and entrepreneurs of the future. It is a great privilege and a powerful position to be in.

As Voltaire said, "With great power comes great responsibility."

It is our responsibility to shape our youth, both mentally and emotionally—to educate them about the world and about life, so they leave our classrooms as strong-minded, clear-thinking people who know what they want from the world, know their worth, and are willing to work hard to achieve it.

Secondly, what Thinking Globally, Acting Locally means is that we need to realise we are not just a very large island. As John Donne said, "No man is an island." We need to think big—bigger than our country, bigger than our continent. We need to use what we have locally to reach out globally and, conversely, use what is available globally to improve what we have locally.

This can be achieved through modern technology. Through it, we can access the world. What does this mean? It means we have the best minds of the current world and the best minds of the past all at our fingertips and ready to access. It means we can open big doors for our students by allowing them to use global knowledge to find solutions for local problems.

This means that students and educators alike have the ability to find solutions to local problems globally. Teaching children to source answers globally will be one of the greatest things you can do for them. Nothing is new under the sun, so there should always be an answer to the problem.

It becomes a two-way street. You can find solutions for problems, but we have a wealth of knowledge that the world has not previously had access to, which we can now share.

Use technology to allow your local students to think globally and help them to realise that Africa is as close to anywhere in the world. Any information is just one click away.

CHAPTER 5

Nuts and Bolts

Cognitive, Affective and Psychomotor Domain

Dr. Benjamin Bloom created a taxonomy of education way back in 1956, covering the cognitive, affective, and psychomotor domains in education. He believed that all three areas need to be addressed in order to create a well-rounded student.

> ➤ *Cognitive* pertains to the mental stimulation and learning area.

> *Affective* refers to the emotional well-being of students.

> *Psychomotor* covers their ability to put what they think into action, be it verbal or written.

I would like to see more emphasis put on understanding the domain of value, what we call the affective domain, coupled with the psychomotor, where what we learn is translated into action. Not so much on pure academic work and playing back what we have learned without analysing, synthesising, and coming up with new ways of doing things.

I would implement this by, first, getting the force of our current teachers in school on board. We can't do anything as heads of education facilities, if we don't have the backing and support of our teaching staff. Together, we are a mighty force; alone, a principal is a feather in the wind.

I would look very critically at the syllabus we have in teacher training colleges. For instance, in Uganda several years back, we had what we called the Namutamba System, which involved children's education integrated in rural development. That project was done, reviewed, and ended there. I would like to see more of that. That is, you get the three things—your head, your hands, and your heart—involved in what we call holistic education.

There is a need for the government to facilitate service training. (I think we used to have that here.) Don't put teachers in schools and just leave them there for ten years, teaching the same things they did when they started. We need refresher courses to keep current the teaching syllabus and ways of teaching.

For example, we have science integrated into other subjects. However, students who go on to university are not coping because the universities want them to have mastered chemistry or physics as a separate subject. They do not have a sufficiently in-depth knowledge base to move from integrated science to studying chemistry or physics at a university level.

We need to separate the subjects. Teach chemistry on its own, teach biology on its own, teach physics on its own. Subjects work holistically together but need to be taught individually. You don't, as an adult in the work environment, say let me now use my chemistry, my mathematics, or my physics. No, it is one cohesive education that creates a holistically educated student.

You integrate it, and you use it. You may not be recalling that this is what we did in chemistry. We want to create students who are so comfortable in their holistic education that what they have learned comes to them as and when they need it, not in lines learned on a page. It must be a part of them—part of their thinking, feelings, and actions—not just rote education.

It is like memorising the Koran or the Bible. We lose the trees in the forest. You tell the story of the prodigal son, and you miss why the parable was told and how to apply it in your daily life. That's the gift of these stories: less memory and more application.

Further to this, I believe you cannot test someone fully on something that they do not understand, even if they have learned it. There is a vast difference between being able to tell you something and explaining why it is. Students need to be able to demonstrate, whether it is verbally or physically, that they can apply the knowledge they have learned. That is when holistic education—cognitive, affective, and psychomotor domain—have all been well executed.

Let's break down these three critical elements of holistic education:

1. Cognitive Domain

Addressing the cognitive domain moves learning away from giving students facts that they have to learn by heart and then simply write down in exams for the student to pass the subject. Cognitive education sees a teacher being able to explain, engage, and enthuse his/her students in order for them to be able to comprehend the topic, evaluate it, understand it to the point of being able to discuss it, and add their thoughts and ideas to it. It creates an understanding of the subject to the point where a student can move laterally from it and view it from different perspectives and comprehension. It is about understanding the core of a subject, not just the ten facts about it.

Then it takes another step forward. It brings about a cognitive recognition, to be able to explain it to someone else in such a way that *they* understand it. It means being able to apply knowledge to other areas and to link areas, due to an ability to connect subjects by areas that are not always immediately apparent, but which become apparent, after thinking beyond the core topic, subject, or area.

By creating cognitive awareness, the teacher can also discuss the principles of why this area is the current or past, right or wrong school of thought. It creates thinkers, understanders, and students who learn to reason, question, and answer their own questions through thinking about something logically, practically, and thoroughly.

2. Affective Domain

Affective domain is something I have found missing often, not just in students but also in adults. The questions asked under the affective domain are ones that show what we are emotionally made of and then bring to light areas that need work.

By highlighting this area, we bring to the fore our emotions, strengths, and weaknesses. Therefore, we can work with them to create a stronger, more capable person who can be a motivator, educator, and leader in life.

Everything we do is motivated by how we feel. How a subject makes us feel motivates our views and actions toward it. By creating a platform for students to discuss not just the how and the why of a subject, but the what—the motivation behind it, the human factor—we allow them the chance to discuss who they are and what they believe. We teach them, then, that what they believe and how they feel about something is going to direct what they write, say, and do.

Let's use abattoirs as an example. Meat-eaters accept them as a part of being able to put meat on your plate and have a healthy diet. Vegetarians and vegans feel they are inhumane and believe there are better ways to kill animals or advocate even not killing them at all.

This is an emotional subject. By bringing something like this to the fore, the meat-eaters will have to examine how they feel about having their cattle killed; it will motivate some understanding as to why it is necessary. They will then have to counter the vegetarians' arguments and points.

This stops students from merely accepting things as fact because they are written in a book or spoken by a teacher. They evaluate their own standpoint and substantiate their point of view, which brings in cognitive reasoning. They may even have to go and research their position.

There are seldom right or wrong answers, but being able to access your emotions and emotional thoughts about something, verbalise them, and substantiate an opinion brings about a far greater learning experience than rote learning does.

Ethics, morals, and societal norms can be brought into education to teach a broader version of every subject.

3. Psychomotor Domain

Psychomotor domain covers the ways in which the information we have learned and how we feel about it affects our behaviour. It links back to affective domain; the question of how we act within our moral and ethical boundaries, and if we feel good about our actions.

What we do, what we say, and how we feel comprise who we are. We accept that as adults, so we need to teach that to our students. This way, they are well grounded in who they are as people and know themselves before they face the adult world with its multitude of stresses.

If you can teach a child to think, reason, evaluate, and act based on those foundations, you will have an adult who can lead, motivate, learn, and accept responsibility for their actions. Is that not what we want from the people we deal with in life? Is that not what we want from our leaders, educators, and employers?

We need to teach our students to think for themselves, not just accept what is taught to them. They can then reason and work out if they accept something, and then match their actions accordingly.

Civic Education

So often, scholars go through school in a bubble and do not interact with society. Civic education brings the student and the outside world together, showing the student why being an active participant in their communities is important for holistic well-being.

Once students leave school, they will immediately be thrust into society as adults.

Giving them civic education on how the world works, how their country runs, and how it affects their communities and themselves allows them an insight into the nuts and bolts of how the world functions.

When we look back, we recall that we used to have things like handicraft. We used to have things like civic education, what we called civics. There was less emphasis on passing exams than we do now.

We didn't have a lot of examinations right from pre-school to kindergarten going to P1, not regular tests like you see now. People go to school and the first thing they do is take an exam. We give them a term exam. Then, we have in-between midterm tests and also end-of-term exams. So much time is spent on testing and data collecting, I don't think there's time even for correcting, examining, and rearing students as to how to answer those questions. This is not how to solve problems of today and tomorrow.

Some time back, there was an attempt to have what you call, for lack of a better term, technical education in general education. That's why, if you went to Mengo Senior School, you would find they teach electricity and electronics, along with metal work and carpentry. They teach home economics and technical drawing, either geometrical drawing or building drawing.

Now, students who studied the so-called mathematics used to talk of bearings. When you go to geography, you also talk of bearings. That's where you have the link. So, a teacher should not only be confined to being the so-called specialist in a subject. She should see how to relate geography to history and mathematics. You can't do contours or map reading when you are not applying your mathematics.

So, *how* you teach is very important, just as important as *what* you teach. Perhaps even more important than what you teach. So, we ask the questions: what to teach, how to teach it, when to teach it, and why to teach it. It is important to teach the links between school subjects as well as between those subjects and the world out there. It is vital to teach children to look for the links and to be able to draw from one area for another area's solutions.

Civic education is about linking knowledge with the real world and with life. These are precious gifts to give a student, ones that will keep giving to them forever.

I strongly believe that a syllabus belongs in the hands of someone well-prepared and someone with broad ideas of what education is all about.

Education comes from the Latin word *educare/educere*, meaning to demonstrate, to show the way. To educate is not to pack people's heads with so-called ideas or facts. It is showing them the way; to show is to demonstrate how things are done.

For example, why do we have a rift valley there? You can see there's the history of it, and there's also the geography of it.

It is useless, if you are going to teach history, just to give your students a lecture on the history of Uganda, the partition over Africa. or the American Revolution without actually discussing what brought it about, what happened during it, and what its effects were on the people. We have to create a whole story, not just the bones. We have to flesh out subjects and then give them hands that link them to other subjects.

Where do you partition it? Now, if we are going to talk about the Industrial Revolution, why don't you look at it not only in Europe, but come down, even, to Africa? If you talk about the movement of people, migration, didn't people move in Europe? So, you would look at migration, at people moving from one place to another everywhere. It's not only happening in Uganda, Kenya, or South Africa.

You may find the same reasons, or you might look at what common themes arise, if you were taking history. Agrarian Revolution—where? In Uganda? Where? What is common? If we are going to talk about wars, what are the causes of wars or revolutions? What does the French Revolution have in common compared to the American Revolution? If people were asking for bread and one said, "Give them a cake," what was the revolution about in America?

What are the apartheid problems about in South Africa? What about what happened in Australia, the Maori Wars, what were they about?

So, if we do not separate these things, you can use not only textbooks but also novels. If one was teaching the history of South Africa and you used the novel by Alan Paton, *Cry, the Beloved Country*, it would give a different perspective. I think perspective of oppressed and oppressor, of left or right, of leaders and led, is something that should be discussed, as it gives a completely different perspective and a more holistic understanding of a situation.

Very importantly, we need to teach children to think for themselves, not just accept what we think. We need to teach them to think, reason, evaluate, and substantiate. You can't do this in one midterm test and end-of-term exam.

Continuous Assessment

Continuous assessment is the term used for a system that evaluates a student's progress on a continuous basis, rather than a single exam. Many students do well in class but don't do well on exams. This may be for many reasons, which we will discuss in this section. Continuous assessment allows for work to be assessed on an ongoing basis throughout the academic year, giving a better overview of the student's capabilities than one exam would.

If we read the Policy Review Commission Report, there were some recommendations that were even accepted by the government in the white paper. One of them is continuous assessment. Continuous assessment will require us to develop a profile for an individual student, so you can see how that individual student is progressing.

No one is sending a child to school to compete with another child, but we do put more emphasis on ranking. What was your position? Number one. You don't look at what your score was on a particular mathematics test; you look at the position. It is possible they failed because they had outside circumstances that affected them on that day, however they were also number one.

So, that's what I am putting emphasis on: recruiting and re-training the teachers. Even the way they ask questions can be rethought. There is some area where they may say, okay, this is a take-home exam. Or another where the educator gives the student four questions, for example, and they then go home with the questions and prepare. Then, in the examination room the next day, the students know the material we want them to report to us about.

It is not as simple as it sounds. In fact, it can be very difficult, as it may show the student that they don't know the answer, which means they have to research it. They may come to the examination room prepared to write, but on re-reading the questions, after having time to think about it, they realise they want to answer it differently. What we have found with open book tests is that students take the time to look for answers accurately and do not just write the first thing that comes to their minds. They think, revise, evaluate, and only then write an answer.

This is a much more holistic and cohesive way to gain understanding, rather than just being able to answer a question that is asked. What it does is change the way of revising and studying. The student not only finds his answers himself, but he gains a better understanding of why a question was asked in a certain way and, if it was asked in that way, what answer is necessary.

There was one other thing that developed in the Uganda education system; I see now it's no longer very popular. They used to put out model answers. There were people who would write model answers. What this did was cause a lot of students to fail, because they could give you the right answer, provided the question was asked exactly as it had been stated. However, if it was phrased differently, students had no understanding of the concept of what was being asked and could not answer the questions.

If you teach to give understanding and teach the students how to study to gain understanding, you are likely to get students who pass with flying colours.

Continuous assessment is about evaluating the students' performance throughout the year, not just giving a pass/fail verdict based on one exam. Perhaps a good student, one who should have passed well, has had some family tragedy that sees them failing the final exam dismally. Is it then fair, based on one bad day, that they are forced to repeat an entire year of schooling?

I think not. Students should be assessed continuously, and this, in conjunction with exams, should be the foundation on which the student's final year-end mark is based. This is a fair way of evaluating a student's knowledge of a subject, rather than only what they can remember on one day.

That is the gift of holistic education: it combines head, heart, and hands together, using cognitive, associative, and psychomotor domains.

This process gives the teachers an opportunity to teach understanding. The students learn to think for themselves about a subject, and they are able to work from a point of complete understanding, not just spout facts they have been spoon-fed.

CHAPTER 6

Educating Thinkers

Why Learning to Think Out of the Box is Paramount

The people who achieve much are those who think outside of the box. When people are encouraged to think about and rationalise what they are told, their minds start working in different ways, and creative solutions and ideas come to the fore. This is a far cry from rote learning, where students simply memorise what they are taught in order to be able to spew out an answer for the end-of-year exam. It creates minds that can turn a problem around, search for possible solutions, and rationalise the answers they have come up with.

These are the people who are going to make a difference in the world. This is what holistic education, using cognitive, affective, and psychomotor domains, teaches students.

Being able to think laterally, or out of the box, if you will, allows a person to step aside from a challenge or problem and search other areas for solutions. Why we use a box for this analogy is that a box is useful but limiting. A box can hold a lot of things but not everything. It confines the person to what is in the box; it does not allow them to seek answers in the entire world outside the box. You will not find the mathematical answer to what two plus two is in a box filled with air. However, if you step out of the box and find plants growing, you can take two of them, add another two and get your answer.

Whilst this is a very simple example, it clearly demonstrates the point I am trying to make. Outside the box, the world's knowledge and experience is at your fingertips. Inside the box is just your own personal knowledge and experience.

As I said in the previous chapter, holistic education is combining the head (thinking) and heart (emotion), and it allows you to then use your hands (action) to execute the solutions you have found.

People who think out of the box are the ones who actively seek solutions in all areas. They do not sit and wait for an answer to be given to them. They have enquiring minds that ask: What if?

"What if" is such a powerful mental tool to have. It doesn't mean every answer to "what if" is the right solution, but it means you are using your creativity and cognitive skills to explore different avenues that could lead you to an answer.

Thinking outside the box means you don't discredit possible solutions, no matter how off the wall they seem to be, until you have evaluated them thoroughly.

Societal norms see in-box thinkers. Society teaches people to accept that the norms dictated by advertisers, leaders, movies, and such are the only way. The people in life who have created the greatest changes are those who have rallied against what was seen as the norm and sought alternate solutions.

Ghandi, Leonardo da Vinci, Martin Luther King, Nelson Mandela, Madame Curie, Einstein, Thomas Edison, the Dalai Lama—all these people and so many more did not allow the box to be their life. They knew things had to be different, that there were solutions that may not appear currently, but were out there somewhere.

They just had to find them. They had to keep searching for answers other than those that were fed to them.

Think about what our youth faces right now. They are bombarded with what to wear, what to buy, what to do, what to listen to, what to think about—all these things try to create in-box thinkers. Advertisers don't want people to think for themselves. They don't want kids to think the latest pair of trainers are just another pair, much like the last ones. They don't want them to think it is ridiculous that wearing a certain brand of cologne is going to draw women to you or that using a certain mobile phone is going to make you popular.

Free thinkers are the ones who change the world because they are not bound by the norms of the world. They use their own cognitive reasoning to rationalise that it is not up to a mobile or a pair of trainers to get them where they want to be. It is up to them and the hard work they are willing to put in.

This is the other side of out-of-the-box thinkers: they are hard to control, and society likes to control people.

Creating people who think out of the box from school level will create people who don't just slot into the rat race of life. It creates movers and shakers, motivators, and passionate leaders of tomorrow.

What a privilege this is for us in the education field: we get to shape the adults of tomorrow. Let's give them the very best tools we can, so they are capable and able to lead the world in the strong, clear, and forward-thinking way that comes from living outside the box.

Thinking outside the box sparks creativity and allows people to find creative solutions to problems. It allows them to view the world holistically and see that everything is linked, with each link being the potential solution they are looking for.

How to Teach Students to Think for Themselves

Educators are often of the "I speak; you listen" ilk. By having discussions on the topic being taught and encouraging discourse about it, the educator allows the children to think for themselves and educate themselves on new ideas. It creates knowledge and understanding, not just absorption of facts.

Our educators can use what they have learned to bring about intellectual thinking in the classroom. This happens when educators think holistically about education, not simply narrowly thinking about the subject they are teaching.

You can't say one thing is technical and another is academic. Some people think they are academic and that those who make chairs are not academic. But now, how do you make a chair when you don't use your mathematical brain? You cannot think that people who study technology are less able academically, because, without academics and in-depth knowledge, there can be no technology. I'm calling for integration of knowledge and no fragmentation. We need to change mindsets from "I am/you are" to "we are."

We need to accept and, more than that, be respectful of everyone's talents. One person may be very good mathematically but unable to put his knowledge into practice, whereas another person may be practical and able put the mathematician's knowledge into practice.

When we stop thinking about different levels of academia, we will see that all areas of study and knowledge dovetail. Thinking outside the box allows you to utilise every person's knowledge, because you are not thinking that they have nothing to offer.

Let me tell you something I have learned in my many years of dealing with people: every single person has something of value to offer you.

You cannot work, think, and act outside the box if you have prejudices. They will limit you and limit your solution-finding abilities. Therefore, affective domain education allows a student to work through these areas in a safe environment. While students are still forming ideas and ideologies, we have them in our classrooms.

What an amazing opportunity: to form free thinkers and people who accept that everyone has value. Also, that every talent is a worthy one and everyone in every field of expertise or passion is of value.

Let me tell you what will happen if we do *not* educate our students to be holistically minded. They will think in small boxes and not believe the outside world has any value, whether this be their fellow man or people from other countries.

We need to think globally and act locally. Are we educating people to live their lives in their villages, towns, or cities or to remain in their country for the rest of their lives? Or are we educating them to be able to think and be a progressive and proactive part of the world?

We need to teach our students that the world is a click away, because, with the Internet, Skype, and Facebook, with Twitter, Snapchat, podcasts, TEDX Talks, and so many other platforms, we need to be prepared and educated to think and function on the same level as the rest of the world.

Technology has made the world as small as one town, and everyone in the world is your neighbour, so people need to know how to communicate with and utilise their neighbour's skills.

If we don't create students who think for themselves, who don't embrace technology, who don't think outside the box and accept people's differences as strengths, not abhorrent weaknesses, we will raise the next generation who have no skills to function in the global markets. In not embracing change and holistic education, we stand to stall the growth not only of our youth, but of our country for the next twenty years, until someone effects change.

That is the harsh reality. *We* have to do it, or else *who* is going to? With great power comes great responsibility. I have said that before, and I will say it again.

Our power as educators of the next generation of adults means we have a great responsibility to not educate them as we were educated. There may have been nothing wrong with our education for our time, but that time has passed. It is a fast-paced, different world we are thrusting upon our graduates. Our responsibility is to give them the right tools for the world as it is today and also the skills to utilise every tool available to them, so they may go forth and be creative and successful.

As a parent, think about how proud we are of our children when they are happy and successful. As educators, each child in our care is our child, and we should want each and every one of them to succeed just the same as if they were our own flesh and blood.

shutterstock.com · 279303704

How to teach students to think for themselves:

 **Allow discussion and brainstorming**

 **Teach students to listen to ideas that are contrary to what they believe**

Analyse emotional response

Take things outdoors

Look to different areas for solutions

Read a book about someone in their area of interest

Encourage creative thinking

***

There are so many ways that an innovative educator can expand the way their students go about gaining knowledge.

Thinkers, Speakers and Doers

Often, students fall into one, two, or three of the above categories naturally. In holistic education, we need to teach students to be all three. You can't only think and not speak and act, or nothing will ever be achieved. You can't speak without thinking, because that will cause harm and the outcome will not be good. And you cannot act, or do, without speaking or thinking, as your plan will not succeed.

The trilogy of success lies in thinking first, speaking second, and acting third.

Thinkers

We all know people who are predominately thinkers. They don't speak a lot and often suddenly act upon something they have been mulling over without speaking to anyone about it.

This unilateral action based on thoughts cannot succeed to its full potential, as there is no way we can think of every possibility and eventuality in a situation. Thinking without speaking brings about a narrow plan of action.

Why would you not bounce ideas off people you trust? They will give you insights, ideas, and possibilities that you may not have thought of before. Also, they may see pitfalls you haven't thought of, which could save you time, money, and frustration.

However, thinking has to be the first step in anything you do. We need to train our students to think first, speak second, and act third. Any successful person will tell you how they spent months, possibly even years, thinking about their plan before they spoke to people about it and put it into action.

Critical thinking is vital, as it teaches the student to employ creative thinking. By teaching students to think for themselves, they learn to have faith in their creative ideas, research it, analyse it looking at pros and cons, and lastly, they learn to formulate the ever-important step-by-step process and plan that will get them from having an idea to implementing it.

The problem comes in when students don't feel as if they are being heard, so they stop speaking about their ideas. Educators can offer a safe environment in the classroom that allows free thinking. There should be a support base that does not allow ridicule of ideas that seem somewhat *avante garde,* but instead gives the student the opportunity to explain their rationale and how they see the plan working.

The greatest inventions in life all started with a thought. Teaching students to think out of the box, to think creatively, and to follow that creative thinking through, no matter how off the wall the idea is, will expand their minds. It will allow them to stretch their knowledge, even if the ideas come to nothing. It will make them more knowledgeable. What it also does it teach them to allow themselves the freedom of thought.

Whilst this is something we do, as adults, oftentimes children are put in a box by society, by family rules, and by their peers, so they don't feel they should be thinking about anything other than the next exam, the next sports match, and their homework.

It is the thinkers who hold the potential to change the world.

Speakers

Some people seem to be born with the ability to speak. They speak to anyone at any time. It is a gift, but like all gifts and talents, it needs to be used wisely.

The positive aspect of being a speaker is that you always have something to say. The negative is that it may not always be something worthwhile.

This is where training students to be thinkers first before being speakers is so important. Thinking before you speak allows you to only say what is good, what is right, and what you can substantiate.

As an educator, you will have to learn to motivate the thinkers to speed up and speak and do. But conversely, you will have to teach the speakers and the doers to slow down, stop, and think.

If speakers do not think about what effects their words will have, they may cause offense and set into motion something they never planned on starting.

Teaching students that thinking before they speak or act allows them to back track, if their ideas don't pan out in the way they expect. The process of thinking first gives them an out, an exit, and no one is the wiser.

Because speaking comes so easily to them and thinking about what they say is slower to happen, their words can also cause problems for them and hurt other people. An educator will find that the trickiest students are the speakers, as they have an answer for everything.

The speakers in the classroom tend to dominate the room, as they always have something to say. This can overshadow the thinkers, who are slow to speak, or the doers, who don't always know how to verbalise what they know they can do.

Instead of discouraging them and breaking their outgoing spirits, educators need to teach speakers to channel this verbosity in the right direction. Drama, school plays, and leadership motivation are all areas where educators can allow the speakers to thrive without their overshadowing the quieter thinkers.

Doers

The doers are always an easy collection of students. If you need something fetched, they will do it. If you need something done, made, or someone helped, they are your person. Whilst this is an asset to the classroom, always allowing the doers to do means that the other students don't get to participate as much as they should.

The doers are always full of energy and this should be harnessed and used at the right times. These are your athletes, dancers, and sports students.

But there will be thinkers and speakers who also have skills that may be overshadowed by the powerful enthusiasm of the doers.

Without action, nothing is possible. Without thought, nothing will succeed. And without speaking, a complete use of resources is not achieved.

As educators, we have to admit that the doers are a benefit, because it takes the burden of all action from the teacher. By teaching the doer to think first, you will take them out of their comfort zone and start them on a different creative process.

When you ask a doer to do something, perhaps ask them *why* you think they need to do it, what their plan of action is, and what the outcome will be.

***

We all live very comfortably in our comfort zones. We rely on what we are good at and use that to overcome areas where we are weak. In holistic education, we endeavour to create well-rounded students. Working on weaknesses is as important, if not more so, than working on strengths. If we can strengthen the areas where the student is weaker, we are bringing up a notch their level of education, knowledge, and, yes, power.

Being an educator is a balancing act and, I think, one of the most important jobs in the world, as you are readying a child to the very best of your ability and for the rest of their lives.

Training educators in holistic education will give them the skills to draw words from a thinker, to show a speaker the benefits of thinking first, and to help the doer find the words and thoughts to plan their actions.

The nuts and bolts of education is taking a student and helping them grow into the best, most knowledgeable, capable, strong, kind, and active version of themselves in the time you have with them.

It is about seeing potential in each student, working with them to balance their strengths and weaknesses, and mostly, creating a sense of self that they can be proud of. As an educator, the actual balancing implies restraining and letting out, because you don't want either the speaker, doer, or thinker to be the domineering person. They all have to be given the opportunity to be expressive, which comes from what they have thought, done, or spoken in their different ways.

This will lead to their being adults who know how to think, reason, analyse, plan, verbalise clearly, gain support, and then act on their initial ideas.

That leads to creative adults who will go out into the world confidently and successfully. We, as educators, have then done our job well.

CHAPTER 7

The Art of Leadership

The Qualities of a Good Leader

We all know of good leaders and bad leaders. For me, the quintessential difference is that good leaders lead from the head and the heart, and bad leaders only lead from the head.

The difference is connection with the people they lead and connection to their inner core of personal ethics. The difference is, when a person leads only with their head, they may make good analytical decisions, but they don't take the human factor into account. I believe the human factor is a major part of being a good leader.

The qualities of a good leader are:

* **Integrity**
* **Passion**
* **Commitment**
* **Trustworthiness**
* **Humility**
* **Vision**

Integrity

Integrity is a word we all know. It has the obvious meaning of being a person who holds themselves to a certain set of moral principles. What I find interesting is that its root is from the Latin word *integer,* meaning intact. For me, that is the best explanation of integrity: one whose moral compass is intact. If your moral compass is intact, you will follow it, and it will lead you on the straight-and-narrow path to do what is right, not what is easy.

Integrity means you follow your own principles, even when they are not popular or when it would be easier and often more beneficial not to.

Integrity is a quiet quality that permeates every aspect of your life. You will deal with people fairly and justly and take into account their circumstances before making a judgement, because you understand that everyone is going through something, and whatever they are going through may cloud or alter their actions.

Integrity is about having a strong set of principles that you follow: to do what is good, what sits right with your soul, and to treat others as you would want them to treat you.

Another definition of integrity is to be complete and whole. Usually, this is used for inanimate objects—it may be a fabric that has integrity, meaning it is strong and of good quality. This can also be applied to people. A person of integrity is strong and has good qualities. They are whole and complete, because they act in a way that brings them peace within.

If you treat people and yourself with respect, you will have inner peace, as you are acting in a way that you feel comfortable. It is only a person who has no moral fibre who can act badly towards others and feel nothing.

The third definition of the word integrity, again not usually used on people but still very relevant, is "complete, unified, and of sound construction." I don't know about you, but I would want anyone whom I trust to lead me to be complete, unified to their cause, and of sound moral construction.

Integrity in a leader is of paramount importance, as the leader will have their own code of conduct and act on it accordingly. They will be honest, decent, respectful, trustworthy, faithful, committed, and want to work towards the greater good of the people they lead, by putting themselves second.

Start looking at world leaders, and see if you can spot the ones with integrity and those without. The ones who have integrity change the lives of people they lead for the better. They are the Nelson Mandelas, the Mother Theresas, and the Mahatma Gandhis of the world.

Integrity is first on my list of the qualities of a good leader. A person who has integrity will naturally have the other qualities that will see them doing what is right for the people they lead, not what is fashionable or will get them votes. They lead because they care. They do right because their integrity, that integral set of principles by which they govern themselves, will not let them do anything less.

Passion

At its core, passion is about deep enthusiasm. It is about being excited, motivated and enthused about something. I don't know about you, but I want my leaders to be enthused about the potential of what they can achieve for their people due to their position.

Passion's great depth of emotion will lead people to want to do better for the object of their interest. It will see them seeking ways to make the other person's life better, sparking creativity of thought and ideas.

Passion is about being focused and determined to not only do what is right, but to do what is the very best for people, because it means so much to you.

A leader who lacks passion lacks enthusiasm and drive. They lack emotional connection with their people and lead by rote, not by motivation, to see their people better off.

Being passionate about something means you will give your time and resources to ensure that the object of your passion is left in a better way or place than before.

I want that in a leader. I want a leader to work tirelessly and use every resource they have at their disposal to make our lives better. A country that feels appreciated by its leaders and feels that the leaders listen, understand, and try to help them is a country that works harder, that leads better lives, and is more productive. With all of this, the citizens feel they are not just another cog in the wheel of the economy.

Being passionate about the people you lead will find you thinking of new ways to make their lives better and solve their problems.

Passion is the emotional drive of a leader with integrity. It is the fuel that floods through the engine and fires the motor into action. If you are not passionate about something, you will not really care if change for the better occurs or not. You will not feel motivated to action to create change. That is why passion is one of the vital parts needed in a good leader.

Commitment

Commitment is a wonderful thing. It is about being dedicated, connected, loyal, and devoted, and about having allegiance to something.

A person who is committed to a cause or a person or a group of people will go out of their way to do what they can for them. It is about feeling connected to a cause and staying the course through the ups and downs. When the going gets tough, the committed rise to the occasion.

I love to see people who are committed. It brings about the best in them. They will put in extra hours, think of creative solutions to problems, and do what it takes to further the cause to see a better result.

Commitment transforms a leader whose work is a job into one whose work is their life. A committed person will put in those extra hours to get it right. They will spend time thinking about how to solve problems and how to get the job done, because it is important to them. Leaders who have an integral passion for their people will be committed to doing everything in their power to better the lives of their people.

When I speak of leaders, I am not just speaking of presidents and government. I am speaking of every single person in a leadership role.

Whether you are a CEO, a headmaster, a teacher, a parent, or a student, lead with your heart, using your head, and act with your hands. Be committed to what you are leading, because you have been given a great gift of trust that should never be broken. Always remember that hard work has never broken a bone.

Trustworthiness

How many times has someone said to you, "You can trust me"? That always makes me wary. If you have to tell me you are trustworthy, then you are not confident that I will see your trustworthiness by your actions.

I don't want you to *tell* me that you are trustworthy. I want you to *show* me that you are trustworthy.

I want other people to tell me that they know you are trustworthy through their dealings with you.

Trust is a glass vase. It is a beautiful thing. We can confidently fill it with water as we believe in its integrity. When trust is not honoured, the vase drops and shatters. Then, it can never be mended, so it will never be confidently believed in again, even if it is glued back together.

Personally, I think it is the greatest compliment when someone trusts me, be it with their children to educate, the students who come to me with their problems, my staff who believe in my ability to lead them, and the school or my friends and family who know I will do what I say I will.

Trust is precious and should be treated as the ethereal thing that it is. It is not something to be taken lightly. People who believe they can act badly towards another person and still have that person believe in them are sadly mistaken.

Trust is a precious gift. A leader, parent, teacher, or any person should always hold it close to their heart and treat it with the respect it deserves.

Humility

Humility is the balance of being proud of your achievements but knowing that you have a lot to learn. It is about not sitting on your laurels and patting yourself on the back when you do something good, but it is about knowing that no one achieves anything alone. Every success is carried to the finish line by many other people, and we are indebted to them for everything we achieve.

There are always people who get you where you are going, and humility is about remembering them, acknowledging them, and knowing that, even if you are at the pinnacle, there are many others under you and around you, holding you up.

Vision

Proverbs 29:18 says that, without vision, people perish. This is not literal dying because you don't have good ideas. It is about stagnating as a person because you don't think out of the box.

Vision is used to describe sight and aptly so, because it is about seeing potential around you. It is about seeing and seeking solutions, not right on your doorstep, but as far afield as is necessary.

Having vision sees people thinking globally and acting locally, because they see the whole picture of how we fit into the world. Without vision, leaders will only think of today and now. They will not think about creating platforms for the future. They will not seek out answers and assistance from others.

Richard Branson is described as a visionary. What a compliment that is. He is a man who has never let life, circumstances, or people stop him from achieving what is thought to be the impossible. He sees the end that he wants to achieve, and he is passionate about it, committed to achieving it, determined, and focused. That is why he has achieved such success. He is a great leader of himself, and those types of people fire up others to want to succeed.

This brings me to my last point in this section. The greatest leaders are those who themselves show honesty, integrity, commitment, passion, vision, and humility. If you hold yourself to those standards, you will go far and lead well.

Leading so Others Follow

The difference between a leader and a dictator is that people want to follow one and are forced to follow the other. Leading is about living a life that others want to emulate and having characteristics that others can admire. Leading is a responsibility and should not be taken lightly, as the lives of those who follow you are in your hands.

Leaders are not only heads of state or corporate magnates. They are everyday people working nine-to-five jobs. They are parents, students, and teachers. They are you. You have the opportunity to be a good leader, wherever you are and whatever you are doing.

Lead by example—be your best self every day. Work on allowing the qualities that make a leader shine from you, and people will be drawn to you.

Leading so that others will follow is about making people feel a part of the programme. In a school environment, it is about a democratic sharing of responsibility so that one person is not loaded with all the decisions. It is about empowering people, all people, to join in and work together to find solutions and implement them. It is about bringing out people's potential and giving them your trust. *This* is how you lead to help others grow.

Leading means that you are a motivator, visionary, and friend. It means you stop to pick up those who have fallen, and you run with those who are ahead. It is about seeing the people around you as the vital parts in your story that they are. Everyone is in your life for a reason. Everyone has something for you in them. Sometimes, we have to learn a hard lesson that you can't blindly trust people or that some people have their own agenda. But mostly you will find that every person around you has something worthwhile to offer. Never dismiss anyone, as in doing so, you miss an opportunity to learn from them.

True leaders don't have to put others down to gain ground for themselves. They lift people up with them as they go. They don't have to have the best ideas; they just have to have an idea, a vision, and be willing to walk the walk and talk the talk, going alone if necessary. However, people like leaders. They like people who have vision, passion, commitment, and humility, and who are trustworthy.

A true leader will always have followers, if not for the same cause, because they connect with them on a sub-level. This level is where they see a person being the best person they can be and want to learn from them.

Leading so that others will follow means you have to lead from the front. You have to be involved, have tenacity, and believe in your ability to achieve your goals.

Remember the teacher I spoke of earlier in the book, who would come to school in work clothes so he could work in the gardens with the children? That is a true leader. He didn't sit in his office and watch. He got out there and got dirty alongside the children. He wanted them to do something, so he did it himself.

How many times do we see leaders sitting in their plush offices while others do their hard work for them? That is not true leadership. If you are not willing to do something yourself, don't ask others to do it for you.

I want anyone reading this book to understand that leadership means being a servant. It means serving the people you lead. I want that concept to be the challenge in our nation, our schools, our businesses, and our homes.

To be a leader, you should be humble. Knowing that you are not better than the people you are going to lead, but that there must be a leader, and if it is going to be you, then you will do it with integrity, commitment, and humility.

Another thing is knowing that the people you lead have the potential to lead you. The person you are leading can polish your shoes so they shine so well. Everyone you lead has something to offer. That is something we must never forget. We all have different gifts. Every leader needs to allow the people they lead to exhibit their gifts, so they blossom like a flower.

Leadership is not about money, power, big cars, or expensive lavish dinners. It is about thinking of the people you lead as your family and wanting everything that is good for them, not just for yourself.

Leading so that others will follow is not about being at the top or at the front. It is about knowing when you need to be at the front to motivate the people behind you to keep going. It is about knowing when to walk in the middle to listen to the people's stories and problems. It is about walking at the very back to ensure that no one is being left behind.

Leading is about using your head, listening to your heart, and allowing your actions to bring about good change for the people who have trusted and are following you. It is about them, not about you.

Be a true leader and you will always have the help and support you need to achieve your goals.

Everyone is a Leader

Everyone has something to teach others, making everyone a leader. Teaching children that everyone they encounter has a gift of knowledge that can be imparted to them creates students who grow into kind and respectful adults.

We wrongly associate leaders with money. True leaders are wealthy because they absorb knowledge from everyone they meet. They are rich in experiences learned through others' lives. They are rich in compassion, motivation, and dedication. They are rich in heart, because they want to do something that betters others and their lives. That is worth more than money can buy.

Learning that everyone—whether the man I spoke of in the previous section who shines shoes to the street sweeper, the shop owner, the parent, the sibling, the teacher, and the colleague, all of them—is a leader because a leader has a story, a goal, and a plan. Everyone has something to teach you.

I know I have said it before, but I am purposely saying it again. Learn to find the leader in everyone, and you will not only gain immense knowledge of people, but you will gain immense knowledge of yourself.

Lead from within. What I mean is lead yourself first. Motivate yourself, believe in yourself, trust yourself, and let those attributes power you into action. If you see a problem, do what you can to fix it. If you can't fix it, go and get more people involved who can help you. If you lead from within, you live a life you can believe in. You can confidently lead others, because you know you have the ability to lead yourself.

The key to leadership is to bring out the leaders in others. Allow them to use their talents and let them shine. Einstein said that everyone is a genius. But if you judge a fish by its ability to climb a tree, it will spend its whole life believing it is stupid.

A true leader allows others to shine as well as themselves.

CHAPTER 8

Head, Heart and Hands

Holistic education is all about working with all three areas of head, heart, and hands to create a well-rounded student. It starts with leading a holistic life. You cannot educate or lead people in a certain way if you are not living that way, yourself. Therefore, understanding what a holistic life is important.

It is not about anything more than using your head, heart, and hands to guide you. By incorporating all three, you will have a balance in life that you cannot achieve by only using one or two of these core principles. Think of it like a tripod. It is a study piece of equipment, but try and make it stand with only one or two legs, and you will see how vital all three legs are.

The same thought process applies to the Three-H Principle.

Head

Let's first look at how to use your head in life, then we will move on to how to use your head in education.

Without thinking, as we discussed in Chapter 6, you are going to be a headless chicken running around creating chaos wherever you go. You always have to stop and think before you speak and act. This gives you pause to check if you are on the right track or whether you are going to hurt yourself or someone else by your subsequent actions. I am not just speaking physically; most damage done to people is on an emotional level.

The words we use and the actions we take can cause as much and often more damage to someone than a physical action. Therefore, think before you act out of your emotions.

Now, on to education.

Education's main focus has always been on knowledge. Teaching so that children gain knowledge is an important part of an educator's work. However, teaching so that the students understand what they are learning is far more important. When a student understands the concept of the subject, their knowledge will grow exponentially, because they will want to know more about it.

Teaching students the ability to harness critical thinking will allow them thought processes independent of the core subject. They will be able to think on their own, because they have an understanding of the subject. This will allow them to branch off and start thinking out of the box, harnessing creative thinking.

It is a many branches tree that all starts with imparting knowledge and not just facts.

If I say to you that oil floats on water, you may say, "Yes, I know it does." However, if I ask you why this is, unless you have understanding of the molecular differences between oil and water, you will not be able to answer me. That is the difference between knowledge and understanding.

Knowledge is power, and creating a love of knowledge in students means they will want to carry on studying once they leave school. How educators bring about a love of knowledge is all in how a subject is taught. It is about bringing a subject alive through firing up the student's critical thinking mechanism and allowing discussion and debate in the classroom.

What a wonderful place to learn to listen to other people's thoughts without having to try to persuade them that yours are right! What an amazing skill to teach students—that they have the right and can speak up and debate anything. This is a skill that will stand them in good stead when they leave school, much better than just knowing facts.

Being taught to ask what, who, why, when, and how is something they will be able to apply to their lives every day. It will teach them to think and question things for themselves and not just take what they are being told as fact.

It also teaches them to trust their own knowledge and to question things that don't seem or sound right. If an educator stands up before their class of students and says, "It snows at the equator," those students who don't apply critical thinking will believe them. Those who do will say, "Hold on! The equator is closer to the sun than the poles, and the poles are covered in snow, therefore it should be hotter at the equator than at the poles. So no, it won't snow at the equator."

Another student may say that he lived in an equatorial country and his experience is that there is no snow there.

I use this example to show how allowing debate and dialogue in a classroom brings the children from rote learners to thinkers.

Using your head is the first step to success, because it is where knowledge, ideas, questioning, and reasoning begin.

Heart

This section is three-fold. First, it will focus on the individual. Second, on the teacher and their need to teach with heart—that is be passionate about the subjects they teach. Passion motivates others; the best way to foster the love of a subject in a child is to be passionate about it.

Third, it will focus on an educator working with their students holistically, in that they have to realise that what happens at home or on the playground is going to affect the child in the classroom. Having a heart and seeing students as people with lives that impact their work will give the educator a deeper understanding on how to work with their students.

Let's start with how we, every one of us, need to do everything with heart.

Having heart means you allow your emotions to be a part of your decisions and actions. It also means you do things bravely, even if you are afraid. You must have heard the saying, "That person has heart." It means they felt strongly about something and allowed that to be taken into consideration when auctioning their thoughts.

Secondly, and one of the focuses of this book, is how to bring heart into education. An educator who is passionate about their work will always bring more to the classroom than one for whom the job is just a job. We've all had a teacher who was enthusiastic about their work; it brought the subject alive.

Passion brings life and motivation, whether in the classroom or in everyday life. We have spoken about passion in a leader. This translates into the classroom in the same way.

A teacher is leading their students to greater knowledge and understanding of a subject. What better way than to teach it with passion? To find interesting facts and open discussion about it will motivate the students and reach them on a level of emotion, rather than just head knowledge.

Lastly, people need to understand that everyone has problems, adults and children alike. Taking into account that students' home lives will and do affect them at school will help educators be more compassionate about late homework or work not done. Educators need to work holistically with their students and see them more than just seat occupiers. They are people who have families and responsibilities and lives that aren't always easy.

Compassion and teaching with heart will bridge the gap between educator and student and will open the door to communication that may change a student's life for the better. Sometimes, they may feel overwhelmed with trying to balance home responsibilities and school work. By listening and understanding, a teacher may stop a student from buckling under the pressure and leaving the school system.

Also, when a student doesn't understand something, having compassion and not just writing them off as stupid will see the educator looking for solutions for the student in the form of extra tuition and help, to get them to the point of understanding what is being taught.

Educating with heart takes trust in your students. It allows them to take leadership roles in the class so they can develop their skills in a safe, controlled environment. By doing this, they learn what actions lead to good results and what actions lead to bad results. The aggressive student will find that the team he leads won't do as much for him as his counterpart's, who is kind to his team. Through this, he learns to be less aggressive and to assert his strength towards positive and not negative motivation.

What this does is teach children responsibility and how to deal with their peers. This is a good skill to have once they reach the workplace. Not everyone is going to be your friend, but you have to get the job done. So how to do it in the most effective, efficient way that still allows you to be included in the football match at break?

When you create teams out of your students and get them to choose a team leader, the feeling of responsibility for the team is enhanced, as the leader has not been picked by the teacher. They have essentially been elected by his peers, and you will see how seriously the student takes the responsibility. This method also creates bonding between the students; they have to work together to achieve success. These are good skills to learn at a young age, so they can be implemented in the adult world.

To teach with heart is harder than teaching without heart, but the rewards are great. It will be seen in the faces and outcomes of the students, as well as in their enthusiasm for not simply being in a class but being a necessary part of a class where their input is valued.

Heart is the jam in the middle of the holistic sandwich. It is pleasant to find and enjoyable to have. Be the jam, have heart, and see the dynamics of your classroom change.

Hands

We all need to act, or nothing would ever be achieved. Brilliant thoughts are useless if they remain just thoughts. Action is thoughts and feelings in motion.

Acting brings about change, and change is the only motion that can bring goals within reach.

I have spoken to many people who have great ideas, revolutionary even, but they lack the gumption to act on them, and therefore nothing changes in their lives. A thought without action is a dead fish in the water—no use to anyone, especially not to the fish. You have to think about your goal, assess how you feel about it, and find your passion, and then plan how you are going to achieve it—act on it.

A very well-quoted maxim is, "BE the change you want to see in the world." Not *think* about it, not *discuss* how you feel about it. BE it. Act on the change you want in your life, in your community, in your school, and you will then see a change. Thinking about it is good, but without action, it is not going to go anywhere. Be the change, be the feet, be the leader who breaks ground boldly.

Taking this thinking into the classroom is simple. Ask yourself what you would like to see changed in your class and through your interactions with the students. Do they seem to be lethargic and disinterested? Action a field trip. Do they not seem to grasp the understanding of plant growth? Get them to plant their own beans.

Reading and learning bring knowledge. Doing creates understanding. Bringing action connected to the syllabus into the classroom will bring about a greater understanding of the work. Taking the work out of the classroom for field trips will also enrich the students' understanding. We will look at ways to allow hands to work so heads can learn.

Combining head, heart, and hands is the core of holistic education. It sees the educators and the students as beings with their own thoughts, ideas, and feelings, and it works to bring about a strong cohesiveness between all three Hs.

I have seen this principle in action. I have used it myself. It works, because it reaches everyone on a human level. The teacher does not remain a remote individual who stands at the front of the class, reciting facts. The student is not just another seat filled. The engagement between teacher and student comes alive when the student is seen as an individual and the teacher as a person with whom the student can engage.

Holistic education is a way to prepare students for the world after school. It teaches them how to engage, how to discuss, and how to make their own way in a world in which they are no longer a student with a teacher as their buffer between them and the outside world.

If we don't teach our students the necessary skills to cope in all areas, not just in education, how can we say that we have done a good job?

Holistic education also connects students with the community they are going to be living and working in. It teaches them that everyone has value, to find the value in everyone, and to learn what people have to teach them. It teaches them to think, to question, to understand, to feel, and to move.

These are skills that every person can benefit from, and what better way to teach them to our youth? They can then go out into the world as complete individuals and not feel as if they have been thrown from the safety of the school system into the cold, hard world. They will be able to see the world for the bright place that it is, filled with opportunity for those who know how to think out of the box, find their niche, and create a life for themselves, not just a living.

Holistic education encapsulates learning, emotional wellness, and physical condition. Within this framework, it deals with spirituality, understanding, self-awareness, growth, and learning to set goals and achieve them, both individually and as a member of a team.

For me, that is a well-rounded education, one that will create a student who is ready and able to go into either tertiary education or the working field well equipped. That is the beauty of holistic education and why I am such a great advocate of it.

CHAPTER 9

Five Golden Principles for Life

Everybody has golden principles by which they live their lives. These are principles they want to impart to others. As an educator, I wish I could pass on wisdom and what I have learned from life. The only way I can do that for students and others is to live my life to the principles I uphold—leading by example. For me, the five main principles are:

- ❖ Honesty
- ❖ Integrity
- ❖ Determination
- ❖ Hard work
- ❖ Thinking outside the box

Honesty

If a person is not honest, then nothing else he does or says has any credence.

William Shakespeare wrote, "No legacy is so rich as honesty," and I agree. Why is this so important? Without honesty, a person cannot be trusted. Without trust, he cannot be believed. If he cannot be believed, he is just a hollow vessel.

An honest person will always be trustworthy, because they will not lie to you about their abilities or what they think can be achieved. Truth is the greatest respect you can give someone, as hard as it is sometimes to give.

Be a man or a woman of your word. This is not as easy to do as it is to write. Being a person who does what they say they will do is often difficult and inconvenient, but that should not make it impossible.

You need to ask yourself a question: what type of legacy do you want to leave behind? One of a person of good, strong character, who could be trusted to keep his word and help people wherever they could? Or someone who followed their own path and didn't care if they lied, cheated, and stole to get what they wanted? I know which one I want, and I do whatever I can to be the best me I can be.

Being honest creates strength of character, as you will have to find solutions in order to fulfil what you said you would do. It allows people to believe you when you say you will do something, because you can be counted on.

Being honest means, you show people that you respect them and don't want to belittle them with a lie. Honesty is hard to do, as it is much easier to give a "white lie" that will get you off the hook or out of doing something you don't want to do.

Just because something is difficult or takes you out of your comfort zone does not mean you should not do it. People don't grow in their comfort zones. It is only once they are pushed out of them that they are forced to stretch mental and emotional limbs to find new grip holds that will lead them to new places within themselves.

An honest person is not concerned with winning friends by pandering to them. They stand their moral ground and do what is right. This earns them the respect of the people who matter—their families, friends, and colleagues. They would rather do something that may be unpopular but is right than go along with the crowd just to please everyone.

Children are curious, and by making a decision to be honest with them, you will gain their respect. They know when you are skirting the truth anyway, as they have an innate sense of truth, something that I always admire.

The last thing I want to make note of is this: when you are honest, you feel good about yourself. That is a fact. You feel terrible when you lie to someone, no matter how small the lie, and so you should.

They came to you because they trust you enough to ask your opinion or advice, and by telling a lie, even a white lie, you are letting them down and insulting them.

Try the Truth Test, and see how much better you feel when you tell the truth and then have the opportunity to explain why you are answering the way you are. People who count will listen, even if the answer is not the one, they want.

Integrity

Even though I wrote about integrity earlier in the book, I feel I must add what it means to me. I couldn't leave it out of my principles, as it is too important.

For me, integrity means that I say what I mean to say, this being what I believe. It may not always be well received, but I am not going to say things that go against my beliefs to appease someone else.

I have a personal code of conduct that I follow; do what is right, not what is easy. Be a man of good morals and a man of my word. I believe God watches over me, and I want my conduct to reflect that I am a man whose faith guides his path.

C.S. Lewis said that integrity is doing the right thing even when no one was watching. I agree with that, because integrity is not about what others think about you. It is what you think about yourself.

Integrity is an alignment of your values with your actions and thoughts. This makes you strong, inwardly and outwardly. When you speak of structural integrity, you speak of the strength of a building or structure to be able to withstand wear and tear and forces of nature. It is the same with personal integrity: you create a strong core and strong actions that align with each other, and then you are able to weather what life throws at you, because you don't have to wonder if you are going to get caught up or your lie is going to be exposed.

Integrity creates freedom and personal peace.

Determination

I am determined about many things. I am determined to be a man of integrity, I am determined to give my best in whatever I do, and I am determined to work hard towards what I want to achieve.

In this way, I am no different than most people.

Determination is about being committed to yourself and your goals. It is about being committed to the people around you and committed to weathering the ups and down with them.

Determination is about being firm in your purpose, whether that is to be a good, honest person or stick to your path until you achieve your goals.

I have seen many educators in my time who are determined to make a difference in their students' lives, not just to while away the time until the end of the scholastic year. These are the people who are remembered by the students long after they leave school as having had an impact on their lives.

Being determined means you are committed to seeing something through to the end. You understand that it may not be easy, that you are probably going to want to give up at some point, but you know you won't. This is because seeing through whatever it is to the end is an accomplishment in itself, as well as receiving the reward of achieving your goal.

Determination will change and shape you. It will make you a better person and a more resilient one. When you have committed to something, gone through hard times but not given up, and then reached your goal, you will realise you are capable of much more than you thought you were.

Hard Work

I am known for saying that hard work breaks no bones.

I believe, if you are going to do anything, do it to the very best of your ability and give it everything you have. Otherwise, you are just wasting your and everyone else's time with a half-hearted effort.

If you are going to do something, you may as well do it well, with determination and commitment, because what happens when you do something half-heartedly is, more often than not, you have to re-do it. Then you have spent double the time doing something that could have been finished long ago.

As educators, we are conditioned to give time frames for work. Projects, homework, exams—they all come with time frames.

What I want to tell you is something I taught my teachers and students: time management is bound to success. If you manage your time well, you will never be rushed or late. You will show respect to others by being on time, which says to them that you respect them and know their time is valuable.

Bound to that is hard work. Manage your time and work hard at whatever you do, and you are certain to succeed.

A wise man said to me, "Whatever is worth doing is worth doing well." Give it your best shot, your all. That way, you can never fail; you can only learn and grow.

Nothing comes from nothing. Hard work is vital to achieve anything. If you don't want to work hard, don't bother starting, but it is your loss. You lose the chance to experience life, to grow, and to achieve something that will make you stand a little taller and be proud of yourself. You and your life are worth putting in the hard work.

Whether you are an educator, parent, youth, CEO, or any other position you hold in life, be committed but determined, be honest, and act with integrity. Be creative, allow yourself to grow, and you will succeed.

Thinking Outside the Box

This little gem again.

Imagine if we did everything as it had always been done. There would be no advancements, no change; nothing new and exciting would ever happen.

The changes in the world are made by the dreamers, because they don't listen when people tell them it can't be done. They are so far out of the box that they have forgotten what it even looks like.

Live big. Think big and act boldly. If you accept there is no failure in life, only lessons to be learned, then there is no reason not to try anything. The world is there to be conquered.

If you feel as if something is not working in your classroom and you are not connecting with your students, try something completely different. Get out of thinking small, as small thoughts have small outcomes.

Seek solutions that are far from the norm. Seek answers that make you think, "That is crazy, but it may just work!" Look for ideas and solutions that excite you. If you are excited about an idea, you will convey that to others and to your students.

Live your life out of your comfort zone, and see the wonderful and extraordinary world that is out there. Encourage creative thinking from the people around you—your friends, family, and students—and see the incredible things people are capable of thinking.

Life is exciting and stimulating outside the box—step out, give it a try! Let your mind seek ideas that are beyond the norm. I can guarantee you won't go back to the box.

I have had many experiences over the years when I was faced with problems and none of the conventional solutions were working. It was then that I used my golden principles to help me find alternate solutions.

None of us want to be judged, so if a student was branded a bad egg, I would disregard what had been said about them and would tell the student they had a clean slate with me. Their actions going forward would determine how we interacted.

That was out-of-the-box thinking, as many students carry labels from one year to the next without the ability or a chance to change.

Allowing people to be their best selves, regardless of their past, more often than not ensures they grow into being a better person. The growth happens because someone finally believes in them.

Isn't that what we all want? Someone who sees our head, heart, and hands and who wants to help us become our best self?

That is what holistic education is about: growing together as one unit, headmaster, staff, and students, in order to become a family. Learning together, growing together—holistically.

CONCLUSION

The reason I wanted to write this book was twofold. The first reason was to not lose my legacy, especially matters of education. Secondly, to contribute to those in leadership positions in education one or two things that they may keep from my experience.

We must also realise that education begins at home. We should use what we have in the schools, the PTA, to first of all get parents to understand how to prepare and make their children ready for school. Even in the olden days, children would roleplay. They may have gone to a wedding and came back home to say, "I am the groom. I am the bride." They used clay to make bowls and played house.

These days, we kill their initiative.

First of all, our homesteads are small. We are now raising kids in tiny rooms with big walls around them. We should let children enjoy playing. Through playing, they pick and try out some of the things we are talking about, so we can get what we call an Aha! moment. That is the moment when you discover.

Let them play with the planking, play with anything out there, and encourage them. Don't say they are wasting time. Encourage children to learn through play and experience life themselves.

So, home education for parents is important, because if there's a mismatch between what the school does and what happens at home, it will be very difficult for us to have these reforms we are talking about. Let PTA meetings not just be about money. Let's also have open days, so parents come and see what children are doing in school.

There's already a finding, and it's true, that children of parents who actively participate in school activities tend to benefit more from schooling than those parents who send their children "to whom it may concern." So, let us have a link between home and school, and that may help us to have the reform we are talking about.

There's this question of parenting. We all grow up and have children, and we are, for the most part, unready to be parents. Some of us think to be a parent you simply need to find the funds and send your children to school. We forget that children learn from what they see.

They see, they hear, they do. Much of what children bring to school is from what they have learned from home. How do we get parents responsible enough to be active participants in the education of their children?

I want to propose we use parent's associations to help—for parents to help each other. To form the family, we spoke of forming within a school.

I want to see parent families as much as I want to see students acting like families. We need to support each other as guardians, parents, and educators of the children in our care. We can also help out those young parents.

When they first send their children anywhere, they are very anxious. It is hard for a parent when they have sent their firstborn to school or day care. They pack their bottles and so on, but they may not even know where this food will be kept. The government of Uganda says, "Let children carry food from home." I don't know how many homes can afford packing children's food for school lunch, as well as feeding their family on a daily basis.

The majority of children in schools go without lunch, and this concerns me. I want to see change, because I want to see things happening that benefit our children and our youth.

This is my passion. These children are our future, and we need to give them the very best that we possibly can give them. Make them strong intellectually, caring and aware emotionally, and fit and healthy physically. We can't do it alone. We need support from the government and businesses. These students are their future workforce; it is worth investing in them.

Another big thing with this reform we are talking about is the question of financing education. Is the government taking on what it can properly afford? Is free education about constructing classrooms and paying teachers' salaries? It goes way beyond that.

We need the government to sit down and do the math to see what it's going to cost to keep one kid in school for a day. To see what it would cost to give each child a sandwich and a fruit juice for lunch. Children can't be educated on empty stomachs. They can't be educated without teachers and without classrooms.

Emphasis needs to be placed on the important things that will make our country a better, stronger place, now and in the future. There is no better place for finance to go than the leaders of tomorrow—our children.

ACKNOWLEDGMENTS

I would like to acknowledge my former student, Mr. Stephen Kasenge, who has been the driver behind the writing of this book. Also, my children, Rachel, Christine, Tom, Esther, and Eva, for their support. As well as Action Wealth Publishing, for publishing this book.

ABOUT THE AUTHOR

Samuel K. Busulwa was born on a bright day in September, at Jungo Maternity Centre as the ninth child born to Mr. & Mrs. Laban and Eva Semagulu. He was married to the late Joyce Busulwa and had 5 children. Mr. Busulwa grew up in a family which believed in the importance of education and went through his school years at some of the top schools in Uganda.

Samuel K. Busulwa was educated at Makerere University in Kampala, where he attained a BA Honours (1965), following it with a Postgraduate Diploma in Education. In 1971, he attained a scholarship through the church of Uganda to Alexandria, Virginia in the United States to do his Master's in Theology. To continue with his higher Education, he was later sponsored by the Virginia Seminary to go and attend Columbia University in New York, where he did a course in curriculum design, development and implementation then later did the same course at the University of Mauritius.

From 1968 to 1970, Samuel was serving at Bishop's Senior School, Mukono. On his return from Columbia University, New York, he was posted to Masaka SS in 1973. In 1976, he was appointed headmaster and then later posted to

Aggrey Memorial School. Between 1985 and 1988, he was transferred to Mengo Senior School as headmaster. Whilst at Mengo Senior School, he was unexpectedly made a headmaster for King's College Budo, where he served from 1989 to the end of 2000.

Mr. Busulwa, being a man of integrity and honesty, serves as a Church Warden in the capacity as a member of the diocese synod and also in the capacity on the council as a delegate to the provincial assembly for the church of Uganda. In addition, he is a member of the consortium court.

Integrity got him elected as the Chairperson of the worship committee that was responsible for the coronation of the current king of Buganda Ssaabasajja Ronald Mutesa Muwenda Mutebi II. In this committee, Samuel was proud of being the Chairman of the Cardinals, Bishops and Arch Bishops who also sat on that committee.

In 2001, Mr. Busulwa was invited by the late Professor William Ssenteza Kajjubi who was vice Chancellor of Nkumba, to become their first full-time Academic Registrar of Nkumba University, where he worked up-to 2009. Given the great work done while at Nkumba University, after retiring there, he was invited by Prof. Right. Rev. Michel Senyimba to Ndejje University to start new courses especially at the Kampala campus. The courses that he started were Computer Science with Education and Early Childhood Education which led to the increase in intake at the University. He served here until 2014.

Education being his passion, despite having left the education system, he started a consultancy that deals with the training of teachers for schools, giving workshops to teachers on management and designing school curriculum. The interest in this came while he was still a headmaster and also a member of the National Curriculum Development Centre.

Printed in Great Britain
by Amazon